Today the Virgin is Present in the Church

Today the Virgin
is Present in the Church
Toward a Byzantine
Liturgical Mariology

Geoffrey Mackey

Pittsburgh, Pennsylvania
2012

For Gabriel and Alexandra

For she is Your mother – she alone –
and your sister with all. She was to You mother;
she was to You sister. Moreover, she is Your betrothed
with the chaste women. In everything,
behold, You adorned her, Beauty of Your Mother.

Saint Ephrem the Syrian, *Hymns on the Nativity*

Contents

Acknowledgements

Any book is the result, not of one person's labor, but of a whole community. In this case, the work grows out of more than one community, each of which has played some role in the theological development that led to this work. The book that you hold in your hands is essentially the thesis which was the culmination of my graduate work at the Byzantine Catholic Seminary of Ss. Cyril and Methodius in Pittsburgh, Pennsylvania. The work that I did there, however, was made possible by an even wider community, ecumenical in scope. So there are many people to thank.

My father, the Rev. Dr. Jeffrey Mackey, first instilled in me a sacramental worldview and introduced me to the beauty of liturgical worship. Larry Tremsky first introduced me to the glories of Eastern Christianity – especially as expressed in iconography, liturgy, and music – which started me on the path that led to the Byzantine expression of the faith.

I must thank, too, my faculty and classmates at the Byzantine Catholic Seminary who, in a spirit of grace and hospitality, welcomed me as a fellow learner. Special thanks are due to the Very Rev. Protopresbyter Stelyios Muksuris and the Very Rev. Archpriest David Petras.

Several people were especially helpful in the production of this project, offering encouragement, editorial suggestions, or direction, especially: Paul Hunter, Lauren Larkin, the Rev. Guy Mackey, Subdeacon Theophan Mackey, the Very Rev. Dr. Justyn Terry, the Rev. Christina Vance, and Derek Wiertel.

I am grateful, too, to Dr. Fernando Arzola, Jr., the Rev. Micah and Stephanie Chisholm, the Rev. Jared and Joni Driscoll, Father Daniel Forsythe, the Very Rev. Archpriest John Petro, Bishop Seraphim Sigrist, the Ven. Dr. Mark Stevenson, and Michelle Wiertel for their friendship and support.

Above all, thanks are due to my wife, Erin, who with patience and grace has supported me as I have pursued theological education. None of this would have been possible without her support. It is to our children, Gabriel and Alexandra, that I dedicate this work.

God grant them all many blessed years!

Introduction

Christian theology is inseparably bound with Christian life. Christianity is a faith lived, a life experienced. Foundational to this faith is the idea of communion, of a spiritual interconnectedness of the believer with the Godhead and with all of the other believers of every time and place. This communion, this union, is expressed in a variety of ways, touching on every aspect of the Christian life: theology, yes, but also morality, politics, commerce, worship, recreation, the arts, and every other human endeavor.

For the Christian Church of the Byzantine tradition, worship is the central expression of the faith. For the Eastern Christian, theology is inextricably tied to its liturgical expression. Theology is more than a mere exposition of propositional truth; rather it is a lived experience of prayer and worship. This is not merely individual prayer and worship, but the worship of the communion, gathered and passed on from generation to generation. "While a Western Christian generally checked his faith against external authority (the magisterium or the Bible), the Byzantine Christian considered the liturgy both a source and an expression of his theology," writes Meyendorff[1]. While this may be an oversimplification of the dichotomy between Eastern and Western theological approaches, what is being expressed is that, in the Byzantine Church especially, one observes the principle attributed to Prosper of Aquitaine: *ut legem credendi lex statuat supplicandi* ("that the law of praying determine the law of believing"). To understand Protestant beliefs, one naturally turns to the various denominational confessions or statements of faith. An obvious source for Roman Catholic beliefs is the teaching magisterium of the Church, today most clearly codified in the

---

[1] John Meyendorff, *Byzantine Theology: Historical Trends and Doctrinal Themes* (New York: Fordham University Press, 1979), 115.

Catechism of the Catholic Church. However, for the churches of the East, experiential immersion is perhaps the most effective means by which one might come to understand the Christian faith. This is the underlying assumption of this thesis.

The liturgy – the whole lived and experienced worship of the Church: the Divine Liturgy, the Divine Office, and other rites – is both formative and informative for the Christian believer. How one prays will shape how and what one believes. In the liturgical churches, an annual cycle of feasts and seasons is observed, thus ensuring that the faithful churchman will be exposed to – and (ideally) participate in – a whole systematic presentation and *anamnesis* of the Gospel which is applicable to his or her life. In it the Church participates in the whole earthly life of Jesus Christ, his most pure Mother, the coming of the Holy Spirit, and the lives of the martyrs and other saints of ages past.

Paul Bradshaw and Maxwell Johnson have recently demonstrated that the understanding of all of these feasts and seasons together constituting a "liturgical year" is a relatively recent one, each piece of the calendar developing more or less independently.[2] Still, the overall effect of this annual rotation of commemorations is to place the sources of theology before the faithful gathered in worship. Therefore one might say that within the whole yearly cycle, the practicing Christian encounters all of the great truths of the faith.

Within this liturgical cycle, Christians of apostolic lineage observe a number of greater and lesser commemorations of the *Theotokos* and Ever-Virgin Mary. Sadly, in the last 500 years, beliefs about Mary of Nazareth have become expressions of the divisions between Christian bodies. Catholic, Protestant, and Orthodox faithful all differ on their acceptance of various aspects of her earthly life and present role. For their part, the Churches of the Byzantine theological and liturgical heritage express their beliefs most clearly within their liturgical celebrations. And it is in these observances that one can most clearly understand what a

---

[2] See Paul F. Bradshaw and Maxwell E. Johnson, *The Origins of Feasts, Fasts and Seasons in Early Christianity* (Collegeville, MN: Liturgical Press, 2011).

Byzantine Christian – Catholic or Orthodox – believes about Mary.

Byzantine liturgies are composed primarily of two sources: biblical texts (both Scriptural readings and paraphrases used throughout the texts of the liturgies) and later non-biblical hymnody. As regards the canonical Scriptures, the Byzantine Church finds the Mother of God present not only in her relatively brief appearances in the Gospels, Acts, and the Apocalypse. She is, in addition, found in an extensive Old Testament typology. She is foreshadowed in the bush which Moses saw was burning but not consumed (Ex 3); in the Ark where God dwelt among his people under the Old Covenant (Ex 25.10-22); in the ladder in Jacob's dream (Gen 28.10-17). The *Akathistos* of Saint Romanus the Melodist includes a number of these types. She is "the sea that has drowned the spiritual Pharaoh (i.e., the devil), the rock which has quenched men's thirst of life; she is the pillar of fire leading those in darkness, the land of promise from which flow milk and honey."[3]

As regards the extra-biblical hymnody of the Byzantine Church, we discover that while much of it is biblically based, other elements are apocryphal or devotional in nature. Nonetheless, Meyendorff explains that in "the final form it assumed in the ninth century … the Byzantine hymnographical system is a poetic encyclopedia of patristic spirituality and theology. Its importance for our understanding of Byzantine religious thought cannot be exaggerated."[4]

Within this hymnographical material, however, Meyendorff makes a distinction between doctrinal content on the one hand and "hagiographical legends and poetic exaggerations" on the other.

> The difficulty in using hymnographical materials as a source for theology lies in the tremendous volume and diversity of the hymns. Of course, the many hagiographical legends and poetic exaggerations found in

---

[3] Hilda Graef, *Mary: A History of Doctrine and Devotion* (Notre Dame, IN: Ave Maria Press, 2009), 101.
[4] Meyendorff, 123.

them can be used only in the context in which they were originally written. The Byzantines, however, obviously understood the difference between doctrinal statements and poetry, for some hymns are explicitly called *dogmatika troparia*; those of Sunday vespers, for example, which were always dedicated to the meaning of the Incarnation in terms of the Chalcedonian definition...[5]

In this study, we seek to identify Byzantine Mariology as expressed by six feasts of the *Theotokos* on the liturgical calendar. They will be discussed thematically, first, by exploring the veneration of saints, in particular the Virgin Mary. Then we will examine her feasts associated with the explicit biblical events of the Nativity of Our Lord and the Annunciation. We will discuss the epistle and gospel readings appointed for the Divine Liturgy on Marian feasts. We then turn to the four major extra-biblical feasts of the Mother of God: The Motherhood of Saint Anna, the Nativity of the *Theotokos*, the Entrance of the *Theotokos* into the Temple and the Dormition. Lastly, we will take a brief look at the narrative sources for these feasts, whether biblical or extra-biblical.

Apart from our Lord, no other person has so many commemorations throughout the calendar. We commemorate the many events of Christ's life because in each story we find truth, some facet of our salvation. Everything he did during his earthly life and ministry, he did to affect our redemption. We observe the many events in the life of Mary, however, because she is the archetypical Christian and has preceded us in experiencing the eschatological hope of all Christian people. Hans Urs von Balthasar has written:

> In meditating on her life in all its phases we learn what it means to live for and with Christ – in the everyday, in an unsentimental matter-of-factness that nonetheless enjoys perfect inner intimacy. Contemplating Mary's existence, we also submit to the darkness that is imposed on our

---

[5] Ibid.

faith, yet we learn how we must always be ready when Jesus suddenly asks something of us.[6]

About each of these commemorations of the Virgin's life, we will ask three questions. First, what are the origins of this feast? Second, what is the biblical or apocryphal narrative foundation for this commemoration? Finally, what do the liturgical texts – those appointed to be sung in Church – tell us about the Virgin? In this way we can observe the shape and content of a Byzantine mariology.

Finally, it should be noted that this is not an attempt at a complete mariology. There is still much more that can be said beyond the scope and the scale of this study. There are other commemorations, hymns, apparitions, legends, and icons that could be examined. Some of these will be identified in chapter six. It is hoped, however, that this study may be a beneficial addition to the literature on the *Theotokos* and a step in understanding her from the corporate, liturgical perspective of the Byzantine Christian East.

---

[6] Hans Urs von Balthasar, "Mary in the Church's Doctrine and Devotion," in Hans Urs von Balthasar and Joseph Cardinal Ratzinger, *Mary: The Church at the Source* (San Francisco: Ignatius Press, 1997), 117.

Chapter One
On the Veneration of Saints

Before exploring the role of the *Theotokos* in the liturgical life of the Byzantine Rite, we must first look to the role of the saints in general in the Orthodox/Catholic faith. When examining the piety of an Eastern Christian one notes that the veneration of saints plays a significant role. The most conspicuous action of the *cultus* of saints is perhaps the veneration of icons. When the faithful enter the church, they reverence (bow before) the icons, kiss them, and light candles before them. Icons are carried in processions. These images adorn believers' homes. Furthermore, saints are invoked in hymns and their intercession is requested in prayers. And of course there is the *Menaion* – the cycle of feasts throughout the ecclesiastical year.

For the Eastern Christian, the doctrine of the "communion of saints" is not merely a dogmatic affirmation without a practical application. Like communion with other living believers, it is an ongoing interconnectedness, a union in Christ. Metropolitan Kallistos Ware calls this "a chain of mutual love and prayer; and in this loving prayer the members of the Church on earth, 'called to be saints,' have their place."[7] When an Eastern Christian invokes a saint or an angel, he is asking a fellow believer to pray *with* him. It is an affirmation of the reality of life beyond the grave – even a deeper and more realized life, for to be absent from the body is to be in the presence of the Lord.[8]

THE SAINTS IN GENERAL

The role of saints in general (like that of the Virgin Mary specifically) has been an area of ecumenical disagreement since

---

[7] Timothy Ware, *The Orthodox Church*. (New York: Penguin Books, 1997), 256.
[8] See 2 Corinthians 5.8

the Protestant Reformation. While the Latin Church does not differ significantly from the Byzantine in this regard, the churches of the Reformation have objected – in varying levels of intensity – to the invocation and veneration of the saints. Calvin, in his *Institutes of the Christian Religion* objects forcefully:

> Wherefore, since the Scripture calls us away from all others to Christ alone, since our heavenly Father is pleased to gather together all things in him, it were the extreme of stupidity, not to say madness, to attempt to obtain access by means of others, so as to be drawn away from him without whom access cannot be obtained.... To procure the favour of God, human merits are ever and anon obtruded, and very frequently while Christ is passed by, God is supplicated in their name. I ask if this is not to transfer to them that office of sole intercession which we have above claimed for Christ? ... But if we appeal to the consciences of all who take pleasure in the intercession of saints, we shall find that their only reason for it is, that they are filled with anxiety, as if they supposed that Christ were insufficient or too rigorous. By this anxiety they dishonor Christ, and rob him of his title of sole Mediator, a title which being given him by the Father as his special privilege, ought not to be transferred to any other.[9]

Martin Luther, too, objected to the invocation of saints, considering it "one of the abuses of the Antichrist" (by which he meant the Pope).

> Although the angels in heaven pray for us (as Christ himself also does), and in the same way also the saints on earth and perhaps those in heaven pray for us, it does not follow from this that we ought to invoke angels and saints; pray to them; keep fasts and hold festivals for them; celebrate Masses, make sacrifices, establish churches, altars, or worship services for them; serve them

---

[9] John Calvin, *Institutes of the Christian Religion* (Vol. II), trans. Henry Beveridge. (Grand Rapids, MI: Eerdmans, 1957), 168-169.

in still other ways; and consider them as helpers in time of need, assign all kinds of assistance to them, and attribute a specific function to particular saints, as the papists teach and do. This is idolatry. Such honor belongs to God alone.[10]

Elsewhere he writes, "Of the invocation of saints nothing is said in Scripture; therefore it is necessarily uncertain and not to be believed."[11]

The Church of England officially outlawed the invocation of saints (along with several other perceived abuses of the Latin Church) in its Thirty-Nine Articles of Religion: "The Romish Doctrine concerning Purgatory, Pardons, Worshipping and Adoration, as well of Images as of Relics, and also *Invocation of Saints*, is a fond [i.e., foolish] thing, vainly invented, and grounded upon no warranty of Scripture, but rather repugnant to the Word of God."[12]

Dutch Reformed theologian Herman Bavinck argues, "Holy Scripture does say that believers on earth may appeal to each other for intercession (Num. 21:7, Jer. 42.2; 1 Thess. 5:25), but never mentions asking the dead for their intercession; and both angels and human beings expressly refuse to accept the religious veneration that is due only to God (Deut. 6:13, 10:20; Matt. 4:10; Acts 14:10ff; Col. 2:18-19; Rev. 19:10;22:9).... Even if one grants a general intercession of the saints for believers on earth, it by no means follows that they may be invoked and venerated for that purpose."[13] While these objections are directed against the Roman Catholic Church's practices, they could equally be used against the Byzantine Tradition.

Protestants are, however, by no means unanimous on this account. The Anglican Church has always kept a liturgical calendar which included festivals of saints. Today the Lutheran

---

[10] Martin Luther, "The Smalcald Articles," in *Martin Luther's Basic Theological Writings*. Timothy F. Lull, ed. (Minneapolis, MN: Fortress Press, 2005) , 334.
[11] Luther, "Confession Concerning Christ's Supper – Part III (1528) in *Martin Luther's Basic Theological Writings*, 68.
[12] Article XXII. "Of Purgatory," *emphasis added.*
[13] Herman Bavinck, *Reformed Dogmatics* (Vol. 4) (Grand Rapids, MI: Baker Academic, 2008), 626.

Church, too, has a sanctoral cycle. Still, it might be argued that, while they have *commemorations* of saints, these are not intended to promote the saints as objects of veneration, but as models of Christian life for emulation. Nonetheless, even among Protestant bodies, there are some who would allow – at least optionally – for the veneration and invocation of saints.

Before responding to these objections, it will be helpful to briefly examine what we mean by "saint" and what the goal of the Christian life is. Father Lev Gillet put it simply that "the aim of man's life is union (*henosis*) with God and deification (*theosis*)."[14] This *theosis* can be understood in several ways. One way is that believers become by grace what Jesus Christ is by nature. That is, Jesus Christ is the Son of God (by nature; eternally-begotten of the Father, as the Creed says). In Jesus Christ, and through his work, we may become *by grace* sons and daughters of God and brothers and sisters of Jesus Christ. "But to all who did receive him, who believed in his name, he gave the right to become children of God, who were born, not of blood nor of the will of the flesh nor of the will of man, but of God" (John 1.12).

Another biblical image for *theosis* is the "putting on" or "clothing" with Christ. Saint Paul writes, "But now that faith has come, we are no longer under a guardian, for in Christ Jesus you are all sons of God, through faith. For as many of you as were baptized into Christ have put on Christ" (Gal. 3.25-27).

For some theologies, salvation is best understood as a legal contract. Through the work of Christ, who was sinless, God the Father pardons those of us who are – and remain – sinful. Luther's famous phrase, *simul iustus et peccator* ("at the same time righteous and sinner"), is how righteousness is understood[15]. Because we have "put on Christ" like a robe, God looks at us and

---

[14] A Monk of the Eastern Church, *Orthodox Spirituality: An Outline of the Orthodox Ascetical and Mystical Tradition* (Crestwood, NY: St. Vladimir's Seminary Press, 1987), 22.

[15] This is not to say that there is no theology of sanctification within Protestantism; there is. However, in general, in Protestant theology there is a hard distinction between justification and sanctification. Within an Eastern soteriology, salvation is one and includes both concepts. There is, for the Orthodox Christian, no salvation without sanctification.

sees Jesus instead, and therefore accounts righteousness to us which is not really ours. While this metaphor may be true as far as it goes, the Byzantine Christian would say that the putting on of Christ is indicative of a deeper reality. Rather than simply cloaking an otherwise filthy, sinful person in a robe of virtue, the doctrine of *theosis* teaches that the filthy, sinful one is actually renewed and made clean in his very person. No longer bound by fallen creation, he is able – by the grace of God – to actually be raised to new life. It is not a legal declaration (guilty, but acquitted), but a renewal of heart and mind – an infusion of the heart and mind of Christ into the person. In the Second Letter of Saint Peter, we read that God's "divine power has granted to us all things that pertain to life and godliness, through the knowledge of him who called us to his own glory and excellence, by which he has granted to us his precious and very great promises, *so that through them you may become partakers of the divine nature*, having escaped from the corruption that is in the world because of sinful desire" (1.3-4, emphasis added).

Theosis is, then, this process of transformation; of becoming, by grace, a partaker of the divine nature. Evangelical theologian James Payton, writing about an Orthodox conception of salvation, explains that this "godliness" in Saint Peter's epistle,

> means being 'like God' in some sense. It includes turning from the corruption brought into the world by human sin, as the 'negative' side of this godliness. The way St. Peter describes the 'positive' side of this likeness to God is striking: he calls it 'participating in the divine nature.' This is the goal of the application of salvation, according to the apostle. The Orthodox thus understand *deification* as an appropriate designation for this hope, given the way the apostle describes it.[16]

"To be deified," writes Metropolitan Kallistos Ware, "is, more specifically, to be 'christified': the divine likeness that we are called to attain is the likeness of Christ... By assuming our

---

[16] James R. Payton, Jr., *Light from the Christian East: An Introduction to the Orthodox Tradition.* (Downers Grove, IL: IVP Academic, 2007), 139.

humanity, Christ who is Son of God by nature has made us sons of God by grace. In him we are 'adopted' by God the Father, becoming sons-in-the-Son."[17]

A saint, then, is one who has achieved, to a great extent, this *theosis*. Saints are the faithful departed who have gone on before and who are, therefore, in the presence of God. We know that to be absent from the body is to be in God's presence (see 2 Cor. 5.8). We are further told in Scripture that, when a believer finally beholds God, he cannot help but be changed further into God's likeness: "we know that when he appears we will be like him, because we shall see him as he is" (1 John 3.2). The doctrine of *theosis*, however, does not place this transformation all in the life to come. The transformation into the likeness of God begins now, in this life, whenever one makes the many, little (and not so little) decisions to turn to God. The saints are those who have been participants in this transformative power of God while on this earthly pilgrimage, and have been recognized as such by the Church.

Further, for the Christian, life is not ended at death, but changed. "Everyone who lives and believes in me," Jesus says in Saint John's Gospel, "shall never die" (John 11.26). The departed rest from their labors, yes, but "their deeds follow them!" (Rev. 14.13) In other words, the seeds that the saints sowed on earth continue to grow when they have reached heaven. Furthermore, the saints who surround the Lamb, are interceding for the faithful still on earth.

What, then, can one say to the objections of our Protestant sisters and brothers regarding the *cultus* of saints? First, for the Orthodox or Catholic Christian, saints are not dead members of the Church, but living ones. One might even say that they are, perhaps, *more* alive than those on earth, because they behold God in a way that we on earth cannot. Second, they do intercede for us. As seen above, even Luther admitted that "perhaps" the saints in heaven pray for us. Calvin writes, "let us not imagine that they have any other way of supplicating God than through Christ who alone is the way, or that their prayers are accepted by God in any

---

[17] Kallistos Ware, *The Orthodox Way*. (Crestwood, NY: St. Vladimir's Seminary Press, 1979), 74.

other name."[18] To which the Byzantine Christian responds with hearty agreement. In contrast to Calvin's claim, the saints are not invoked in such a way that jeopardizes the "office of sole intercession" of Christ. Rather, because the departed saints are indeed alive, their office of intercession (which is a conditional one), is a continuation of the intercessory office that all Christians have for one another. "The intercession of the saints for us is always in and through this unique mediation of Christ.... It is in God alone that we have communion with them."[19]

The invocation of the *Theotokos* and other saints in hymns and prayers, and asking their intercession for those on earth, however, is not the extent of the role of saints in the Byzantine tradition. Much of what Orthodox and Catholic Christians do *in practice* seems to border on (if not go over the line into) idolatry. How is one to respond to such charges? What about lifting up, bowing to, or kissing images or relics? And is it not idolatrous to "magnify" the *Theotokos*? To answer these questions, we must look at the nature of the worship of God and distinguish it from other forms of honor.

ON WORSHIP

The word "worship" in contemporary English has come to have a rather narrow meaning. In discussions and arguments over the veneration of saints in popular apologetic works or in conversations, one will often hear a Catholic or Orthodox Christian pronounce that "we *worship* God alone. We *honor* (or venerate) saints." However, in the sixteenth and seventeenth centuries the word worship had a wider semantic range. Consider this line, spoken by the bridegroom to his bride, in the first Prayer Book of Edward VI: "With thys ring I thee wed: Thys golde and siluer I thee geue: with my body I thee wurship: and withal my worldly Goodes I thee endowe."[20] If a Protestant husband was

---

[18] Calvin, *Institutes*, 168.
[19] *Anglican-Orthodox Dialogue: The Dublin Agreed Statement 1984*. (Crestwood, NY: St. Vladimir's Seminary Press, 1985), 37-38.
[20] *The First and Second Prayer Books of King Edward the Sixth*. (New York: E.P Dutton & Co, nd)

thought to "worship" his wife with his body, clearly it was not simply worship which was at stake in the arguments over the *cultus* of saints, but proper worship. For clarity's sake, however, we will restrict "worship," in this argument, to its contemporary and narrower meaning of the honor and reverence due to God alone.

The question then becomes: is it right to show a creature honor and at what point does one honor a creature at the expense of the honor due to God alone (worship)? At what point does veneration or reverence become idolatrous? This is a question that was answered, from a Byzantine standpoint, during the period of the iconoclastic controversy of the eighth and ninth centuries. The presenting issue of that era was not the veneration of saints per se, but the veneration of images. The great champion of the iconodules, Saint John of Damascus was a Syrian monk who was protected from the persecution of the Byzantine emperors Leo III and Constantine V because, ironically, he lived under the jurisdiction of a Muslim caliph. From that perspective, he was able to write three *apologias* for icon veneration. In these he sets out, among other things, a differentiation between types of honor.

> Worship is the means by which we show reverence and honor. Let us understand that there are different degrees of worship. First of all there is adoration, which we offer to God, who alone by nature is worthy to be worshipped. Then, for the sake of Him who is by nature to be worshipped, we honor His friends and companions, as Joshua, the son of Nun, and Daniel bowed in worship before an angel, or as David venerated God's holy places, when he says, "Let us go to His dwelling place; let us worship at His footstool" … Other worship is given to show respect, as was the case with Abraham and the sons of Nahor. Either do away with worship completely, or

else accept it in the manner and with the esteem it deserves.[21]

Here Saint John is setting out, in distinction from each other, absolute versus relative forms of "worship." Or, in contemporary terminology, "worship" is that absolute and unconditional honor which is due the Godhead alone, whereas what we would today call "veneration" is a conditional and relative honor shown to people or places that somehow deserve our respect, on account of their relationship to God. In his third apology he is even more explicit: "Worship is a sign of submission. Submission implies abasement and humiliation. There are many different kinds of worship."[22] He then goes on to expound five kinds of absolute worship (due to God alone) and seven kinds of relative worship. It is of the first of these relative kinds of worship (veneration) that he says, "First of all, those places where God, who alone is holy, has rested. He rests in holy places: that is, the *Theotokos*, and all the saints. These are they who have become likenesses of God as far as is possible, since they have chosen to cooperate with divine election."[23]

> The saints are to be venerated because God has glorified them, and through Him they have become fearful to the enemy, and are benefactors for the faithful. They are not gods and benefactors by their own nature, but because they were loving servants and ministers of God, they have been endowed with boldness before Him. Therefore we venerate them, because the king is given the honor through the worship given to his beloved servants. They are obedient servants and favored friends, but they are not the King Himself.[24]

This is as clear and concise an understanding of the veneration of the saints from a Byzantine perspective as can be given. Note the

---

[21] St. John of Damascus, *On the Divine Images*. (Crestwood, NY: St. Vladimir's Seminary Press, 1980), 21-22.
[22] Ibid., 82.
[23] Ibid., 84
[24] Ibid., 85

conditional nature of such veneration: it is God who has glorified them and not through their own merit.

Another champion iconodule, Saint Theodore the Studite, makes a similar distinction. "Worship is unique, and belongs to God alone;" he says, "but other kinds of veneration belong to others."[25] There are, for Theodore, various kinds of honor we show to various people, depending on our relationship to them. Subjects, servants, and children venerate kings, masters, and parents. And we don't call this worship, or worry that such honor necessarily eclipses the honor that is rightfully shown only to God. Even the Protestant will honor living saints, heroes of evangelism, preaching, or missionary work. The title "reverend" betrays that there is (or at least at one time was) a sense in which the clergyperson was seen to be in a state due a certain amount of honor. To this day those of the Anglican tradition still call their archdeacons "venerable." For the Byzantine Christian, such variations of honor do not end at physical death. The saints are, quite literally, "venerable."

The Byzantine tradition employs different Greek words to distinguish between the worship due to God and the honor or veneration due to created things. *Latreia* is the unconditional, exclusive worship of God alone. The word "idolatry," thus, means the worship of an idol. However, *dulia* refers to veneration of the saints. This is a conditional honor due to something or someone made holy by God. From this we get the word "iconodule," for example, for those who opposed the iconoclasts by venerating holy images. A third word, *proskynesis*, is also used to describe physical acts of veneration such as prostrations, kissing, and reverences.

THE ORIGINS OF THE CULT OF SAINTS

The cult of saints undoubtedly began with the cult of the martyrs. As early as the New Testament texts themselves, the

---

[25] St. Theodore the Studite, *On the Holy Icons*. (Crestwood, NY: St. Vladimir's Seminary Press, 1981), 38.

martyrs and other saints were held in a high regard.[26] However, beyond some archeological indications, there is not a great amount of evidence of the cult of saints in the first centuries of the Christian era. Nonetheless, what we do know is that such veneration first occurred at the sites of the burial of martyrs.[27] Using the martyrdom of Saint Polycarp in the mid-second century as our earliest example, we see that an annual celebration of the life and death of the martyr was held where the saint was laid to rest. The dating of the account of Polycarp's martyrdom is a matter of debate among scholars. But whether one accepts the traditional date (a year after the martyrdom itself) or a later date sometime in the third century, "this account still provides us with a picture of what such martyr anniversary celebrations contained before the time of Constantine."[28] Bradshaw and Johnson note that "clear evidence that within the third century, at least, Christian communities were keeping local lists of martyrs and celebrating the Eucharist at their tombs on the anniversary days is provided by Cyprian of Carthage in two of his letters."[29]

Later, as Christianity became legal and then obligatory, other departed Christians, who had not given their lives by the shedding of blood, began to be venerated as well. In a sermon on Saint Eustathius, Saint John Chrysostom proclaims,

> Don't be astonished if, when I began the sermon and praises, I called the saint a martyr. For in fact, his life came to a natural end. How, then, is he a martyr? In response to your love, I've often said that it's not just the death that creates a martyr, but also the disposition. For often the martyr's crown is woven not just from the way out, but also from the will. Indeed, it's not I, but Paul who gives this definition of martyrdom when he speaks in this way: "I die every day" (1 Cor 15.31). How do you die every day? How can a single mortal body possibly

---

[26] See the inclusion of the martyrdom of Saint Stephen in the Acts of the Apostles 7.54-60
[27] Bradshaw and Johnson, 173.
[28] Ibid., 174.
[29] Ibid., 174.

undergo countless deaths? "Through one's disposition," he says, "and through being prepared for death."[30]

By no means did the early Church's veneration of saints end with simple annual commemorations. As early as the second century, it was common for Christians to ask the martyrs for their prayers.[31] And with the custom of the translation and dismemberment of the bodies of the martyrs (and thus the beginnings of the veneration of relics), their cults began to spread beyond the place of their martyrdom or burial.[32] Within 100 years of the legalization of Christianity, Chrysostom would enjoin his congregation:

> And so, let's constantly spend time visiting them, and touch their coffin and embrace their relics with faith, so that we might gain some blessing from them....Let's, then, walk there with a great deal of faith, with lots of enthusiasm, so that from the sight of these saints' memorials, and from thinking about their contests and receiving numerous, substantial treasures from every direction, we may also be empowered to finish the present life according to God's will...[33]

THE *THEOTOKOS* AS UNIQUE AMONG THE SAINTS

Now that we have looked at the veneration of saints in general, it is time to turn to the *Theotokos* herself. "Among the saints," writes Metropolitan Kallistos, "a special position belongs to the Blessed Virgin Mary, whom Orthodox reverence as the most exalted among God's creatures."[34] Of course, we know from the New Testament, of the unique role that Mary of Nazareth played in the historical outworking of the redemption of the world. In the Scriptures, her primary role is that of the Mother

---

[30] St. John Chrysostom, *The Cult of Saints*. (Crestwood, NY: St. Vladimir's Seminary Press, 2006), 55.
[31] Bradshaw and Johnson, 180-182.
[32] Ibid., 183-184.
[33] Chrysostom, 99.
[34] Timothy Ware, *The Orthodox Church*. (New York: Penguin Books, 1997), 257.

of Jesus and she appears very infrequently. Despite this scant primary evidence, the role of the Virgin grew in the early Church. Apart from the *Protoevangelium of James*, which looked at Mary's life before the Incarnation, (and which we will deal with in a later chapter), the Virgin's role in the early Church was primarily a Christological one. Mary's two primary early titles were the "New Eve" and the "*Theotokos*."

Mary as the New Eve was a theme in several Patristic writers. [35] Just as Eve used her freedom to pronounce a decisive "yes" to the serpent and a "no" to God, Mary used her freedom to say "yes" to God and "no" to Satan. Meyendorff indicates that the Eve-Mary correspondence was prevalent before the Council of Ephesus, when it was superseded by the dogma of the *Theotokos*.[36] Among the pre-Ephesian fathers who used this parallel were Saints Justin Martyr, Ephrem the Syrian and Epiphanius of Salamis.[37]

> By means of this comparison, the early Fathers achieved an important measure of clarity about the Blessed Virgin's function in the divine plan for our salvation. The parallel has a properly soteriological content and demonstrates that the primary concern of the earliest theological reflection about Mary was focused less on her person than on her role in relation to Christ. Mary has a role in relation to Christ, the second Adam, just as the first Eve had a role in relation to the first Adam.[38]

It is precisely this soteriological (and therefore Christological) perspective that gave rise to Mary's other early title, *Theotokos* – a title that is foundational for Byzantine Mariology.

---

[35] Although the fathers drew this Eve-Mary parallel, it has not come down to us in liturgical expression. Joseph Ledit, in *Marie dans la liturgie de Byzance* (Paris: Éditions Beauchesne, 1976), writes that "The parallelism Eve-Mary comes up constantly, but Mary repairs the evil committed by Eve." However, he notes that "I have not found even once the expression 'new Eve,' or 'second Eve,' in our liturgical books," p. 48 [Translation from the French by David Petras].
[36] Meyendorff, 147.
[37] See Luigi Gambero, *Mary and the Fathers of the Church: The Blessed Virgin Mary in Patristic Thought*. (San Francisco: Ignatius Press, 1991), 46-48; 116-117; 124-125.
[38] Ibid., 46.

The dogma of the *Theotokos* (Θεοτόκος) – that is, the teaching that Mary is the "Mother of God," or, more properly, "God-bearer"[39] – was defined at the third ecumenical council, the Council of Ephesus, in 431 C.E. The controversy at hand was Nestorianism, which argued that Mary was the mother only of Christ's humanity and not his divinity. St. Cyril of Alexandria, whose teaching on the matter was adopted by the council, explained that Christ did not take his divine nature from Mary. "Yet, because the Word is hypostatically united to this body, one can say that he was truly born according to the flesh."[40] So this doctrine is not, ultimately a marian one in isolation. It is rather a defense of the divinity and dual-nature of Christ.

Nonetheless Mary, long before the later controversies over her Conception and Assumption, was seen in a unique light among all of the redeemed. No other saint has been dogmatically given a title, for no other saint was as intimately bound up in Christ's redemptive work as the Virgin Mother of God. From a Byzantine standpoint, it is this role – Mary's God-bearing role – which is central. Because of this unique role, the veneration of Mary is given a specific term: *hyperdulia* or "higher veneration." As Byzantine Christians sing week by week: "It is truly proper to glorify you, O *Theotokos*, the ever-blessed, immaculate, and the mother of our God [*Meter Theou*]. More honorable than the cherubim, and beyond compare more glorious than the seraphim; who, a virgin, gave birth to God the Word, you, truly the *Theotokos*, we magnify."[41]

Now, having seen how the Byzantine Church understands the veneration of the saints and located the *Theotokos* as unique among the saints, we can turn to the marian feasts which will provide the foundation of our liturgical Mariology.

---

[39] *Theotokos* is often rendered in English as "Mother of God," which is a sort of dynamic equivalence for "God bearer." It is true that we do not mean that Mary simply "bore" or "carried" God, but bore him *as a mother*. However, particularly in the Eastern Christian context, where she is referred to as both "Meter Theou" and "*Theotokos*" it seems better, for the sake of clarity, to translate "*Theotokos*" as "God-bearer" or to simply leave it untranslated, which I do throughout.
[40] Cyril, *Epist.* 4; PG 77, 48 B., quoted in Gambero, 237.
[41] *The Divine Liturgies of Our Holy Fathers John Chrysostom and Basil the Great* (Pittsburgh: Byzantine Catholic Metropolitan Church *Sui Juris* of Pittsburgh, USA, 2006), 62.

Chapter Two
Biblical Feasts of the Theotokos

Mary's first appearance in the Christian faith precedes even that of Jesus Christ. Although there are Old Testament prophecies which Christians identify as referring to the *Theotokos*, her first explicit mention is in the infancy narratives of the Gospels. Here we read of the Annunciation of the Archangel Gabriel to the Virgin, her Visitation to her cousin Elizabeth, and the birth narratives of the Lord. Although the Visitation has not found its way into the liturgical calendar of the East, the other two events – the Annunciation and the Nativity of our Lord – provide us with liturgical theological content for our Mariology. The Annunciation celebrates the first moment of the Incarnation of the Lord in the womb of the Virgin. And attached to the Nativity of our Lord, and following it on 26 December, is the Synaxis of the *Theotokos*, celebrating her role as birth-giver. It is to these two biblical feasts that we now turn our attention.

The Annunciation and the Nativity of our Lord are temporally connected, the former celebrating Christ's conception and the latter his birth. We will look at each separately, but, as we will see below, the dates depend upon each other, being nine months apart.

THE SYNAXIS OF THE MOST HOLY THEOTOKOS

Preeminent among the roles and titles of Mary is that of *Theotokos*, God-bearer. This role, defined at Ephesus, is the central defining role of Mary. All other marian doctrines make sense in light of this one and all pre-Christian marian typology points to this one. And so it is now that we turn to Christmas, when she gave birth to the Savior.

The Feast of the Nativity of our Lord, Christmas Day, is directly related to the Feast of the Annunciation which is the observance of the conception of the Lord in the womb of the Virgin. Because of her unparalleled role as the one through whom the Word was made flesh, Mary's role is one that is suitably singled out for particular examination and meditation. In the Byzantine East it became customary, on the day following a major feast, to commemorate the persons who played a significant role in the feast. The Archangel Gabriel, for instance, is commemorated on 26 March, the day after we commemorate his announcement to the Virgin. The day after Christmas, the Mother of God herself is commemorated as a meditation on her role at the Nativity of Christ.

This festival of Mary associated with Christmas is the earliest feast of an explicitly marian character. (While 25 March is also a feast of great antiquity, it may have been associated more with the crucifixion of Christ, rather than his conception in the virginal womb of Mary.) [42] Precisely when this feast was observed is a matter of some speculation. Referencing Nicholas Constas, Bradshaw and Johnson note that in the time of Nestorius, Proclus preached a sermon on "the Virgin's festival."[43] But even at that time (mid Fifth Century) it is unknown when this marian festival was being observed.

> While it is a matter of debate which Marian feast is intended by Proclus' reference (Annunciation, the Sunday before, and the Sunday after Christmas have all been suggested), current scholarship has argued that the feast in question was probably the day after Christmas, 26 December, 'a day on which the Byzantine Church

---

[42] See Margot Fassler, "The First Marian Feast in Constantinople and Jerusalem: Chant Texts, Readings, and Homiletic Literature," in Peter Jeffrey, *The Study of Medieval Chant: Paths and Bridges, East and West.* (Rochester, NY: The Boydell Press, 2001), 25-28; Shereghy, 73; Wybrew, 59; and R. Joseph Raptosh, *The Dormition of the Theotokos: A Liturgical Study* (St. Vladimir's Orthodox Theological Seminary, MDiv thesis, 1978), 4.
[43] Bradshaw and Johnson, 205.

continued to celebrate a "synaxis" in honor of the *Theotokos*.'[44]

Constas notes that, "because Proclus' sermon is the earliest indication that such a feast existed at this time, it is probably that it was added to the liturgical calendar by one of Nestorius' immediate predecessors in the see of Constantinople."[45] From Proclus' sermon, we note that, at that time, the theme of the feast was Mary's virginity; by extension, this was a celebration of all consecrated virgins in the Church.[46]

On the other hand, Bradshaw and Johnson note that Proclus' sermon is the first clear reference to such a Christmas-based marian feast. This, however, does not prove that there was *not* such a commemoration prior to the fifth century.[47] Contra Shereghy and Wybrew, they note that "the oldest Marian feast in existence is usually identified as the 15 August celebration of Mary *Theotokos*, having its origins in Jerusalem and first documented in the fifth-century Armenian Lectionary..."[48] Whichever feast came first – the Annunciation or the Synaxis – both seem to have been in place by the end of the fifth century and each commemorating a different facet of the Virgin's role in the Incarnation.

Margot Fassler notes that this first marian feast in Constantinople predated the Council of Ephesus.[49] "The feasts of the Annunciation and of the Assumption had yet to be introduced, in spite of the fact that the 'historical' date of the former was already fixed in some calendars as March 25."[50]

As to the date of the Synaxis, it obviously is directly linked to the date of Christmas. How the date of Christmas is related to the date of the Annunciation, however, is a controversial matter. There are two general schools of thought,

---

[44] Ibid., 205.
[45] Nicholas Constas, *Proclus of Constantinople and the Cult of the Virgin in Late Antiquity: Homilies 1-5, Texts and Translations* (Boston: Brill, 2003), 57.
[46] Ibid., 59.
[47] Bradshaw and Johnson, 206.
[48] Ibid., 206.
[49] Fassler, 26.
[50] Ibid., 28.

each putting forth its hypothesis for how we got the dates of these two feasts. The "History of Religions Hypothesis" argues, following Hermann Usener, that the Church chose 25 December as the date of Christmas in order to displace the pagan celebration of *Sol Invictus*, which had been instituted by the emperor Aurelian in 274.[51] In this case, the date of Christmas would have been chosen first and then, by calculating nine months backwards, one arrives at the date of the Annunciation.

Those scholars, following Louis Duchesne, who adhere to the "Computation Hypothesis" argue that the calculation was just opposite. In this case, it is explained, the date for the Pascha of Christ was first arrived at. Then assuming, as some ancients did, that important historical figures lived a whole number of years, Christ's conception and his death would have been on the same date. Thus, the calculated date of Christ's death would have also been the date of the Annunciation; Christmas would duly follow nine months later.[52]

These hypotheses need not be mutually exclusive. It is quite possible that there was some evidence to support the theory that our Lord was born on or around 25 December *and* that the pagan feast of the Unconquerable Sun played a role in influencing the decision of the Church. Bernard Botte, who favored the History of Religions Hypothesis was "careful to say that the pagan feast had *influenced* the choice of date and not that Christians had adopted the feast, as some earlier writers had been inclined to do."[53] However the date of Christmas was calculated, the Synaxis of the *Theotokos* would naturally follow it.

As one would expect, the content of the Synaxis of the *Theotokos* would be wrapped up in the Nativity/Incarnation theology of Christmas itself. The Nativity According to the Flesh of our Lord and God and Savior Jesus Christ, to give Christmas' formal title, can be found in the canonical Scriptures in Matthew 1.18-25 and Luke 2.1-20. While the Gospels of Mark and John do not include nativity stories, the Gospel of John does begin with a

---

[51] See Talley, 87-91 and Bradshaw and Johnson, 124.
[52] See Talley, 91 ff.; Bradshaw and Johnson, 124-126.
[53] Bradshaw and Johnson, 124.

theological meditation on the Word which was made flesh in the Incarnation (1.1-14).

While the Western Church separates Christmas from the visit of the Magi, the Byzantine tradition includes this commemoration together with the Nativity (as is evidenced by the Magi's inclusion in the traditional icon of Christmas). The hymnody sung by the Church on Christmas includes mention of all of these familiar pieces of the story: the Virgin giving birth, the angels appearing to shepherds in the fields, the wise men visiting the Christ Child, bringing their gifts of gold, frankincense and myrrh. These themes are also found on the Synaxis the following day – in fact, most of the hymnody is the same. Even where it is not the same, however, it is clearly oriented toward the Nativity of Christ.

Therefore, it can be clearly seen that the Synaxis, rather than being a separate feast, is a day set aside for meditation on one particular facet of the Incarnation: the role of the Virgin as bearer of the Word. Romanus the Melodist composed this meditation on this role which is sung at Matins of the Synaxis:

> The mystical Vine put forth the bunch of grapes that was never husbanded, and with her arms as branches she carried Him, saying: 'Thou art my fruit, Thou art my life: from Thee have I learnt that I remain what I was. Thou art my God: for seeing the seal of my virginity unbroken, I proclaim Thee to be the unchangeable Word, now made incarnate. I have known no seed, and I know that Thou art the destroyer of corruption: for I am pure, yet Thou has gone forth from me. As Thou has found my womb, so Thou has left it. Therefore all creation shares in my joy and cries to me: Hail, thou who art full of grace.'[54]

THE ANNUNCIATION OF THE MOST HOLY THEOTOKOS AND EVER-VIRGIN MARY

Precisely when the Annunciation was first observed liturgically is a matter of some debate. As noted above, whether

---

[54] Mother Mary and Ware, 292-293.

or not it was calculated by counting backwards from Christmas or Christmas was calculated by counting forward from the Annunciation, depends on one's conclusions about the calculation hypotheses of Christmas itself. Nonetheless, Bradshaw and Johnson note that "there is no evidence for [25 March] being a commemoration specifically of the annunciation until the middle of the sixth century in the Christian East and only later in the West."[55] A letter written by the Emperor Justinian in 561 claims that the feast originated in Constantinople itself in 550.[56] However, Calabuig indicates that 25 March was considered "a day of mystery" in the West as early as the third century.[57] But this is possibly because of its connection with the death of the Lord. Calabuig writes,

> By a process, the dynamics of which are still not at all clear, of prayerful contemplation on the incarnation of the Word, the feast of the Annunciation evolved. The documentary evidence that has come down to us does not allow us to determine where this happened. In a letter written in 561, the emperor Justinian affirms that the feast was introduced eleven years earlier, in 550, at the time of the reorganization of the liturgy in Constantinople. In the same year Romanus the Melodist composed his well-known *Hymn for the Annunciation*. After the period of Justinian, because of the prestige of the Church of Constantinople and the growing acceptance of the Byzantine rite, the feast of the Annunciation spread to the other patriarchates.[58]

Basil Shereghy also indicates a third century observance of the Annunciation, noting that St. Gregory the Wonder-Worker makes

---

[55] Bradshaw and Johnson, 210.

[56] Bradshaw and Johnson, 210; Ignazio M. Calabuig, "The Liturgical Cult of Mary in the East and West," in Anscar J. Chupungco, *Handbook for Liturgical Studies: Liturgical Time and Space* (Collegeville, MN: Liturgical Press, 2000), 256.

[57] Calabuig, 256.

[58] Ibid.

mention of it. In the fourth century, St. John Chrysostom, too, evidently refers to it.[59]

By 656 it was well established as a feast outside of Constantinople, for a council at Toledo that year objected to its being celebrated on 25 March, as that date fell during Lent or Holy Week. It was felt that such a festal character was inappropriate for the Lenten fasting period. This synod decreed that 18 December should be the day of its celebration.[60]

Ultimately this decision would not win the day, however, when, in 692, the Council in Trullo (Can. 52) reaffirmed the 25 March date, dictating that, whichever day of the week it fell on, it would be "accorded the same dignity as Sabbath or Sunday... and would be celebrated with the eucharist, which was not allowed on fast days in the Byzantine tradition."[61]

To this day, the feast is celebrated on 25 March in both East and West, with the notable exception of the Armenian Church, which celebrates it in 6 April.[62] Because it is both considered one of the twelve great feasts of the Byzantine rite and also falls during the Great Fast, it provides the Church with considerable liturgical complications.

> The pre-festive and post-festive periods consist of one day each. If, however, the feast falls on the Saturday of Lazarus, it has no post-festive period. If it should fall on Palm Sunday or one of the days of Holy Week or East Week, it has neither a pre-festive nor a post-festive period and its celebration is limited to one day.[63]

The content of the feast is, of course, biblically canonical, coming from the Gospel according to St. Luke. Matthew's gospel

---

[59] Basil Shereghy, *The Liturgical Year of the Btyzantine-Slavonic Rite*. (Pittsburgh, PA: Byzantine Seminary Press, 1968), 91.

[60] Thomas J. Talley, *The Origins of the Liturgical Year*. (New York: Pueblo, 1986), 152-153.

[61] Ibid., 153.

[62] Bradshaw and Johnson note that, because of the Armenian Church's differing date, "it becomes difficult to know if this is not, in fact, the earlier tradition in the East" (210-211). This would indicate that it is at least possible that the feast was adopted by Constantinople from Armenia.

[63] Shereghy, 92.

begins with a genealogy and then proceeds directly to the birth narrative of the Lord. Mark begins with the ministry of the Forerunner. And John's gospel begins with the theological meditation on the Word made flesh and proceeds into the Baptist's ministry. Luke alone records for us the narrative of the Annunciation (1.26-38). Graef, writing half a century ago, claimed that "it is now generally agreed that [the stories in Luke] originated in a Palestinian milieu and that their nucleus goes back to Mary herself."[64]

Within the text of the gospel itself, the Annunciation of our Lord to the Virgin appears directly after the annunciation of the Forerunner to Zacharias. A parallel can be drawn between both John's conception and Christ's – a parallel that clarifies the differences between the two miraculous conceptions. In both cases it is Gabriel – "who stands in the presence of God" – who appears to announce the conception (Luke 1.19, 26). In both cases it is a miraculous conception. However, in John's case, the announcement is made to the father of the child: Zacharias. In the case of Christ, it is announced to the mother, for the child has no earthly Father. There are other parallels and differences, as several commentators have noted: Zacharias and Mary are both "troubled" (vv. 12, 29), Gabriel bids them "do not be afraid" (vv. 13, 30), the birth is announced (vv. 13, 31), the addressee questions the angel (vv. 18, 34), and the angel responds (vv. 19-20, 35-37).[65] However the angel's response differs significantly in the two cases. Zacharias is reprimanded whereas Mary is given an explanation. This indicates that Zacharias' question is being raised out of unbelief, whereas Mary's is raised out of awe; this given the reality that Christ's conception – that of very God incarnate – is the greater miracle.

Both announcement narratives are set against the backdrop of various Old Testament annunciations. Raymond Brown identifies five "steps" in the pattern of biblical birth announcements:

---

[64] Graef, 5.
[65] See especially Reginald Fuller, Leonard Johnston and Conleth Kearns, *A New Catholic Commentary on the Scripture* (New York: Thomas Nelson, 1969), 994 and *The New Interpreter's Bible*, Vol. IX (Nashville, TN: Abingdon Press, 1995), 50.

1. The *appearance* of an angel of the Lord (or appearance of the Lord)
2. *Fear* or prostration of the visionary confronted by this supernatural presence
3. The divine *message* ...
4. An *objection* by the visionary as to how this can be or a request for a sign
5. The *giving of a sign* to reassure the visionary[66]

Within this pattern – used by the biblical writers for Ishmael, Isaac, Samson, and John the Forerunner[67] – we now see the greater annunciation of the Word incarnate.

The conversation between Gabriel and the Virgin is a rather simple one, found in Luke 1.28-38. The archangel greets her and she responds with fear. Gabriel then reassures her and announces the conception of the Lord. Mary responds with questioning awe. Gabriel once again responds with an explanation. Mary ends the conversation with her *fiat* and the angel departs. However this brief exchange becomes the kernel of a great many imaginative conversations in Byzantine hymnography.

But the Annunciation to the *Theotokos* is set also against another Old Testament type: that of Eve. In Genesis it is the serpent (often identified in Christian tradition with the fallen archangel Lucifer) who approaches Eve: a fallen angel approaching a virgin. In Luke the righteous archangel Gabriel approaches a virgin. In both cases the approach is unbidden. The serpent does not greet Eve, but questions her (Gen. 3.1). In Luke, Mary questions the angel. In both cases a choice is presented to the virgin which reduces to this: will you act within the will of God or against it? Eve chooses against it: "she took [the tree's] fruit and ate" (Gen. 3.6). Mary, on the other hand, submits to the will of God: "And Mary said, 'Behold I am the servant of the Lord; let it be to me according to your world" (Luke 1.38).

---

[66] Raymond E. Brown, *The Birth of the Messiah: A Commentary on the Infancy Narratives in Matthew and Luke* (New York: Doubleday, 1977), 156. Italics original.
[67] *New Interpreter's Bible*, 42.

The Eve-Mary parallel has its scriptural foundation in the Pauline doctrine of the second Adam: "Since by man came death ... in Christ shall all be made alive" (1 Cor 15:21-22). It was not difficult for the Fathers to perceive the profound connection between the concept of Christ as new Adam and the concept of Mary as new Eve.[68]

It must be noted that in calling Mary the "New Eve," there is not a strict parallel with Jesus Christ's title of "New Adam." While Christ is the new, or second, Adam in that he took upon himself the sin of Adam and overcame it by his *pascha*, the same cannot be said of the Virgin. Mary did not take upon herself the sin of Eve. Rather, she countered Eve's disobedience with her own obedience to the divine will.

In the stichera of small vespers for the Annunciation, this parallel is put into the mouth of Gabriel: "Be not afraid of me, the chief commander of the armies of the King. For thou hast found the grace that thy mother Eve once lost: and thou shalt conceive and bring forth Him who is one in essence with the Father."[69] Later, Mary is given words that again reiterate this parallel: "Lead me not astray, O man, with crafty words, as the crafty serpent once led astray Eve our mother."[70] Jaroslav Pelikan sums this up:

> Here was not only a parallel between the First Adam as "of the earth, earthy," and the Second Adam, Christ as "the Lord from heaven" – thus a contrast between the earthly and the heavenly – but a contrast between a calamitous disobedience by someone who was no more than human, Eve, and a saving obedience by someone who was no more than human, who was not "from heaven" but altogether "of the earth," Mary as the Second Eve. It was absolutely essential to the integrity of the two narratives that both the disobedience of Eve and the

---

[68] Gambero, 47.
[69] Mother Mary and Kallistos Ware, *The Festal Menaion* (South Canaan, PA: St. Tikhon's Press, 1998), 437.
[70] Ibid., 438.

obedience of Mary be seen as actions of a free will, not as the consequences of coercion, whether by the devil in the case of Eve or by God in the case of Mary.[71]

Turning now to the festal texts themselves, we see that the Eve-Mary juxtaposition plays a major role in the hymnody for the day. The Lity at Great Compline place in the mouth of the Archangel Gabriel the words: "Hail, O Lady, thou restoration of Adam and deliverance of Eve,"[72] and "Once the serpent beguiled Eve, but now I announce to thee the good tidings of joy."[73] At Matins we hear the words, put in the Virgin's mouth, "May the condemnation of Eve be now brought to naught through me; and through me may her debt be repaid this day."[74] Hugh Wybrew writes,

> The themes of the texts for the Annunciation come from Luke's account. They are drawn too from the early comparison and contrast of Mary with Eve: Eve who disobeys and so brings about the Fall and the loss of paradise, Mary whose willing acceptance of God's will reverses her ancestor's disobedience.[75]

These themes follow closely the narrative flow of the Annunciation as found in the Gospel of Luke, but provide more poetically evocative language. Much of the hymnody for the day is in the form of conversations between the Archangel and the Virgin. But, for instance, instead of a simple, "Rejoice, highly favored," or "Hail, full of grace," (Luke 1.28) we get a series of more descriptive marian titles and attributes: "Hail, thou pure chariot of the divinity,"[76] "Hail, thou earth that has not been sown; hail, thou burning bush that remains unconsumed; hail, thou unsearchable depth; hail, thou bridge that leads to heaven,

---

[71] Jaroslav Pelikan, *Mary Through the Centuries* (New Haven, CT: Yale, 1996), 43.
[72] Mother Mary and Ware, 442
[73] Ibid., 444.
[74] Ibid., 453.
[75] Hugh Wybrew, *Orthodox Feasts of Christ and Mary: Liturgical Texts with Commentary* (London: SPCK, 1997), 97.
[76] Mother Mary and Ware, 438.

and ladder raised on high that Jacob saw; hail, thou divine jar of manna; hail, thou deliverance from the curse; hail, thou restoration of Adam,"[77] "Hail, thou vessel containing the Nature that cannot be contained... Hail, O Lady, thou restoration of Adam and deliverance of Eve,"[78] etc., in addition to various forms of "Hail, full of grace."

Besides the Archangel's greeting, the other pieces of the Lukan narrative are provided in more ornate form. Mary is troubled: "My mother Eve, accepting the suggestion of the serpent, was banished from divine delight: and therefore I fear thy strange salutation, for I take heed lest I slip."[79] The Archangel reassures her: "Why are thou, O Undefiled, afraid of me, who rather am afraid of thee? Why, O Lady, dost thou stand in awe of me, who stand in reverent awe of thee?"[80] Mary questions how this can be: "Thou sayest that I shall conceive Him who remains uncircumscribed: and how shall my womb contain Him who the wide spaces of the heavens cannot contain?"[81] Gabriel explains: "In His good pleasure shall the Word of God descend upon Thee, as dew upon the fleece"[82] and "beyond words and understanding, in ways that He alone knows, He shall take flesh of thee."[83] And Mary assents: "Since, then, I am purified in soul and body by the Spirit, be it unto me according to thy word: may God dwell in me."[84] These are just a few examples which could easily be multiplied in the hymns of the day.

In addition to recounting the Annunciation narrative in ornamental form, the festal hymns allude frequently to Old Testament prophecies and types. At Matins, Mary is clearly identified by the Archangel as the one foretold in the Law and the Prophets: "It is thou who art prefigured by the utterances and dark sayings of the prophets and by the symbols of the Law."[85]

---

[77] Ibid., 439-440.
[78] Ibid., 442.
[79] Ibid., 450.
[80] Ibid.,450
[81] Ibid., 437.
[82] Ibid., 451.
[83] Ibid., 456.
[84] Ibid., 457.
[85] Ibid., 452.

And Mary herself says, "I have learnt from the Prophet [Isaiah], who foretold in times of old the coming of Emmanuel, that a certain holy Virgin should bear a child."[86] Typological references include the burning bush (Exodus 3.1-6), Gideon's fleece (Judges 6.36-40), and Jacob's ladder (Genesis 28.10-15).

Theologically, the Annunciation – like all marian feasts – is ultimately as much about Jesus Christ as it is the *Theotokos*. This can be seen perhaps more clearly in the Annunciation than some other feasts because of the more incarnational – and therefore Christological - nature of the feast. "Throughout, the texts reflect the dogmatic definitions of the first four ecumenical councils regarding the divinity of Jesus Christ and his relation to the Father: it is the divine Word, the Second Person of the Trinity, who enters Mary's womb and there takes our human nature upon himself."[87] References are frequently made to the paradox of the God whom heaven and earth cannot contain entering into the finite womb of the Virgin. The Father's relationship to the Son is emphasized through the recurring references to the virginity of Mary. Throughout the feast, the hymns are grounded in the truths which are explicit in the Gospel of Luke, but are ornamented poetically, constantly exploring the profound paradoxes of God-made-flesh and virginal motherhood.

As it was noted in Chapter One, it is Mary's role as *Theotokos* which is central to the way the Byzantine Christian understands her. These two biblically canonical feasts of the *Theotkos* – her Annunciation, which is one of the twelve great feasts, and her Synaxis, which is subordinate to another feast – explicitly celebrate this role.

---

[86] Ibid., 451.
[87] Wybrew, 97-98.

Chapter Three
Lectionary Texts for Feasts of the Theotokos

The liturgies of the Byzantine Church are extensively biblical. The Scriptures form the framework of every gathering of Orthodox Christians for worship, whether through direct quotations in the text of the liturgy, paraphrases of biblical concepts, or the public recitation of biblical texts and their exposition by the priest or deacon for the edification of the people. While every Byzantine liturgy is scriptural, the Divine Liturgy – like Eucharistic liturgies of other historic Christian rites – is uniquely composed of two parts – the Synaxis (or liturgy of the Word) and the Eucharist (or liturgy of the Table).[88] The Synaxis (literally, "gathering") was, according to Dom Gregory Dix, "in its Shape simply a continuation of the jewish synagogue service of our Lord's time, which was carried straight over into the christian church by its jewish nucleus in the decade after the passion."[89]

> ...The synaxis normally preceded the eucharist in the regular Sunday worship of all churches in the second century. From the fourth century onwards the two were gradually fused, until they came everywhere to be considered inseparable parts of a single rite... All over Christendom the first part of the Eucharistic action still revolves around the book of scriptures and not around the chalice and paten at all.[90]

---

[88] See Gregory Dix, *The Shape of the Liturgy* (New York: Seabury Press, 1982), "Chapter III: The Classical Shape of the Liturgy: (I) The Synaxis," 36-47 and "Chapter V: The Classical Shape of the Liturgy: (II) The Eucharist," 103-140.
[89] Ibid. 36.
[90] Ibid. 36.

In this first part of the Byzantine Eucharistic liturgy, a lectionary dictates which lessons from the epistles and gospels are read each day of the liturgical year. These lessons are intended, then, to become the subject matter about which the presider or an assisting cleric will preach.

"In the centuries after the death of Constantine, the liturgy became increasingly complex and richly ceremonial. As church feasts were added, passages from the Old and New Testaments were selected and assigned as more or less fixed readings."[91] Today the readings from the Old Testament have largely passed out of the Byzantine Divine Liturgy, though they remain in the Liturgy of the Presanctified and in vigil liturgies of certain major feasts. Nonetheless, an epistle and a gospel are appointed for each day of the year on which the Divine Liturgy may be held. However, the origins of the lectionary are not entirely clear. The authority under which the lectionary was compiled and the scholars who compiled it largely remain largely unknown to us. The Eucharistic lessons for the feasts of the *Theotokos* can be found in Table 1.

Feast	Epistle	Gospel
Motherhood of St. Anna	Galatians 4.22-31	Luke 8.16-21
Nativity of the *Theotokos*	Philippians 2.5-11	Luke 10.38-42; 11.27-28
Entrance of the *Theotokos*	Hebrews 9.1-7	Luke 10.38-42; 11.27-28
Annunciation of the *Theotokos*	Hebrews 2.11-18	Luke 1.24-38
Synaxis of the *Theotokos*	Hebrews 2.11-18	Matthew 2.13-23
Dormition of the *Theotokos*	Philippians 2.5-11	Luke 10.38-42; 11.27-28

Table 1

---

[91] Jeffrey C. Anderson, *The Byzantine Gospel Lectionary*, Introduction (University Park, PA: Penn State University Press, 1992). Retrieved at http://adultera.awardspace.com/SUPLEM/Lectionary1.html. 21 September 2011.

In evaluating the lectionary texts assigned for the Eucharist on the six feasts of Mary with which the current study is concerned, one quickly notes that each feast does not necessarily have unique lessons, distinct from all of the others. Three of the readings repeat on multiple feasts: Philippians 2.5-11 (Nativity and Dormition), Hebrews 2.11-18 (Annunciation and Synaxis), and Luke 10.38-42;11.27-28 (Nativity, Entrance and Dormition). We will examine the readings for each commemoration in turn.

THE MOTHERHOOD OF SAINT ANNA

In the Epistle for the Motherhood of St. Anna, Galatians 4.22-31, St. Paul recounts the Genesis stories of Isaac and Ishmael. He uses this story as an allegory for life under the old covenant versus life under the new. Hagar, Abraham's slave, bears him a son, Ishmael, "according to the flesh," whereas the son borne by Sarah, Isaac, is born "through promise" (v. 23). In addition to referencing Genesis, the author of Galatians quotes Isaiah: "Rejoice, O barren one who does not bear; break forth and cry aloud, you who are not in labor! For the children of the desolate one will be more than those of the one who has a husband" (v. 27; see Isaiah 54.1).

As discussed in the previous chapter, the Scriptures have several stories of barren women receiving the blessing of a child. The feast of the Motherhood of St. Anna, while the subject matter comes from apocryphal sources, is nonetheless in this same scriptural tradition. It thus becomes clear why such a pericope would be used. St. Anna, a barren mother, is, like Sarah before her, granted the late-in-life blessing of a child. And this child will be a child of promise (for the Messiah – and thus the new Israel – will be born from her) just as Sarah's second son was a child of promise (for the Israel would be born from him).

The Gospel for this feast is one of the few places in the canonical gospels where Mary is directly mentioned. First, Jesus talks about lighting a lamp as an analogy for internalizing and incorporating into oneself the teaching that the believer has been given. "No one after lighting a lamp covers it with a jar or puts it under a bed, but puts it on a stand, so that those who enter may see the light.... Take care then how you hear" (vv. 16-18). Of this, Origen writes

> One does not "light" the lamp and conceal it "with a vessel" or put it "under a bed, but on the lamp stand" within himself. The vessels of the house are the powers of the soul. The bed is the body. "Those who go in" are those who hear the teacher [i.e. Jesus.][92]

The lighted lamp, then, is the heart set on fire by the message of the gospel. Once he has been affected, the Christian must not "cover" his faith, but it should be openly proclaimed in word and deed. "Take care then how you hear," Jesus says. The gospel is not for oneself. The Word of God is not for the mere salvation of the individual, but invites the believer into the work of God himself. It is in the context of this statement that Jesus' comments about his "mother and brothers" are made.

Luke places at this point in Jesus' oration an interruption from some of Jesus' blood relatives. They have, apparently, come to visit with Jesus and are unable to get in to see him "because of the crowd" (v. 19). When told of this, Jesus says something that, on the face of it, might appear to the modern reader as insulting. Instead of telling the crowd to make room and welcome them in, Jesus replies, "My mother and my brothers are those who hear the word of God and do it" (v. 21). In other words, they are the ones who do not put their lighted lamp under a jar or a bed. It may appear at first curious that such a text would be chosen for a marian feast. However, on closer inquiry, we see that Jesus is not insulting or disowning his blood relatives. "Now do not let anyone imagine that Christ scorned the honor due his mother," writes St. Cyril of Alexandria, "or contemptuously disregarded the love owed to his brothers."[93] Rather, "his object is to exalt highly his love toward those who are willing to bow the neck to

[92] Origin, *Fragments on Luke 120, 122* in *Ancient Christian Commentary on Scripture: New Testament III: Luke* (Downers Grove, IL: InterVarsity Press, 2003), 135.
[93] Cyril of Alexandria, *Commentary on Luke, Homily 42, Ibid.*, 135

his commands."[94] So Jesus is giving a higher allegiance to those who are his by means of discipleship than to those who are his by blood. Mary, then, is not distanced from Jesus because he is somehow disowning his family. Rather, it is shown that Mary is even *closer* to Jesus than had she been merely his mother. Instead, she is close to him because of her "hear[ing] the word of God and do[ing] it." This can be clearly seen when one turns just a few chapters earlier in the Gospel of Luke and reads:

> And the angel answered her, "The Holy Spirit will come upon you, and the power of the Most High will overshadow you; therefore the child to be born will be called holy – the Son of God." ... And Mary said, "Behold, I am the servant of the Lord; let it be to me according to your word" (Luke 1.35,38)

Mary, then, is great, not merely because she was the physical vessel by which the Christ was brought forth, but because she humbly and unequivocally assented to the Word of God, and took action. That this text should be chosen as the Gospel at the Divine Liturgy on the Maternity of St. Anna indicates an emphasis on the purity of Mary from the beginning of her life.

Both the epistle and the gospel for this feast are shared, as well, with St. Anna's feast on 25 July.

THE NATIVITY & THE DORMITION OF THE THEOTOKOS

The epistle and gospel for the Nativity of the *Theotokos* are repeated again on the feast of the Dormition.[95] Because they are used for both feasts, we will treat them only once here.

The epistle for these feasts, Philippians 2.5-11, is the great New Testament exposition of the divine *kenosis* – the self-emptying of the Lord. The Godhead, which by nature is above all and Lord over all, shows that humility is a divine characteristic by means of the incarnation. The Word of God, one of the Holy Trinity, becomes flesh, subject to all that flesh is subject to, thus

---

[94] Ibid., 136.

[95] The gospel is also used on the feast of the Entrance of the *Theotokos* into the Temple.

showing true humility and giving an example of the Christian life for all who would be his disciples. Of this, St. John Chrysostom said:

> Our Lord Jesus Christ, when urging his disciples to undertake great works, makes himself an example.... This too the blessed Paul does, bringing Christ before their eyes when he urges them to practice humility....For nothing so sustains the great and philosophic soul in the performance of good works as learning that through this one is becoming like God.[96]

This following of Christ in the way of humility is essential to Christian *theosis*, to becoming like God; for, as it is clear from this text, humility is of the very character of God. If Christ our God can take "the form of a servant" (v. 6) and become humble "to the point of death, even death on a cross," (v. 8) the Christian ought also to follow in this way of self-giving sacrifice. "The one *in the form of God* was not stamped by any character other than the Father's, being *a character of the Father's substance*," writes St. Gregory of Nyssa.[97]

Why would such a text be used for the commemoration of the birth and death of the Mother of God? Because it describes her piety and devotion to the Word of God from the beginning of her life until its end. Like her son who took "the form of a servant," Mary shows her own character when she tells the Angel, "Behold, I am the servant of the Lord," (Luke 1.38) and refers to "the humble estate of his servant" (Luke 1.48). Mary, being the archetypical Christian, shows us what it is to imitate the divine character of humility and to submit to the will of God. She is, indeed, the first to imitate Christ's *kenosis* – his self-emptying – in giving birth to him.

The gospel reading appointed for these two feasts also shows us the character of a true disciple and how Mary expresses this character. Luke 10.38-42 tells the story of Jesus visiting his

---

[96] John Chrysostom, *Homily on Philippians* 7.2.5-8, quoted in *Ancient Christian Commentary on the Scripture: New Testament VIII: Galatians, Ephesians, Philippians* (Downers Grove, IL: InterVarsity Press, 1999), 236.
[97] Gregory of Nyssa, *Against Eunomius* 3.2.147, Ibid., 238.

friends Mary and Martha. Martha, who understood that her role was to provide hospitality for Jesus and his entourage, was "distracted with much serving" (v. 40). But distracted from what? It would seem, given the Semitic culture of the day, that Martha was doing precisely what was expected of her. Indeed, that seems to be her own understanding, for she addresses Jesus: "'Lord, do you not care that my sister has left me to serve alone?'" (v. 40).

Jesus' response, far from being what might be expected in such a patriarchal society, is that Mary, "who sat at the Lord's feet and listened to his teaching," (v. 39) had "chosen the good portion, which will not be taken away from her" (v. 42). What are we to make of this? Is Jesus saying that hospitality is unimportant? Far from it! In the Gospel of Matthew, Jesus explicitly claims that one's hospitality has to do with one's ultimate destiny (see Matthew 25.31-46). Rather, Jesus seems to be saying that listening to the teaching of the Lord is the "good portion" in comparison to busying oneself to the point of anxiety over things which are passing. Martha is "anxious and troubled about many things, but one thing is necessary" (v. 41). That one thing is to sit at the feet of Jesus, listening to his teaching. St. John Cassian advises his monks:

> To cling always to God and to the things of God – this must be our major effort, this must be the road that the heart follows unswervingly. Any diversion, however impressive, must be regarded as secondary, low-grade, and certainly dangerous. Martha and Mary provide a most beautiful scriptural paradigm of this outlook and of this mode of activity. In looking after the Lord and His disciples Martha did a very holy service. Mary, however, was intent on the spiritual teaching of Jesus and she stayed by His feet, which she kissed and anointed with the oil of her good faith. And she got more credit from the Lord because she had chosen the better part, one which could not be taken away from her.[98]

---

[98] John Cassian, *Conferences* (New York: Paulist Press, 1985), 42-43.

This is not, of course, a condemnation of hospitality. But, "you will note that the Lord establishes as the prime good contemplation, that is, the gaze turned in the direction of the things of God."[99]

This particular gospel was likely chosen because it mentions "Mary," although certainly not Mary, the mother of Jesus. Quite often lectionary texts are chosen because they contain some key word – "Mary" in this case – which the worshipper is to meditate on. Still, the idea of the *Theotokos* chosing the "better portion" is consistent with what the Church teaches regarding her.

To this pericope are amended two more verses from a chapter later in the Gospel of Luke. The story told here, in chapter 11, verses 27-28, does not actually take place in the home of Mary and Martha (as might be expected if one only heard the gospel proclaimed on these feasts). Rather, it takes place elsewhere, again as an interruption to his teaching. While teaching about unclean spirits, "a woman in the crowd" declares, "Blessed is the womb that bore you, and the breasts at which you nursed!" (v. 27). A statement like this is, of course, nothing out of the ordinary. This would be like saying, "your mother must be so proud!" Truly, the mother of such an authoritative and powerful speaker as Jesus would have to be blessed. But Jesus turns this around in the same way he turned around the discussion of his family in Luke 8.19-21. Jesus' mother is not blessed because she bore him and nursed him, but in the same way that anyone else can be blessed if only they will: "Blessed rather are those who hear the word of God and keep it!" Again, we could turn to the Annunciation narrative to show Mary's fundamental posture toward God's word: "let it be to me according to your word" (1.38).

The use of these texts – both the epistle and the gospel – at both the Nativity and the Dormition of the Mother of God, indicates the Church's belief that – from the beginning of her life (Nativity) to its end (Dormition) – Mary was the humble, self-

---

[99] Ibid., 43.

sacrificing servant of God who loved to hear the Word of God and to keep it in her actions.

THE ENTRANCE OF THE THEOTOKOS
INTO THE TEMPLE

The gospel for this feast is the same as that on the Dormition and the Nativity. However the epistle is changed. The story of the Virgin's Entrance, or Presentation in the Temple, is apocryphal, coming to us from the *Protoevangelium of James*. It is clear that the lesson could not be a direct telling of the story, since only canonical Scripture can be read in the Liturgy. However, the connection of the apocryphal story with the "temple" and "tabernacle" language of the Old and New Testaments is made by the inclusion of Hebrews 9.1-7.

This pericope describes the Tabernacle of the Old Testament with its parts: the "Holy Place" and the "Most Holy Place" (vv. 2-4). In the Most Holy Place was the altar of incense and the ark of the covenant. Under the old covenant, the priests would regularly enter the Holy Place to perform the necessary sacrifices for the people. However, only one man – the high priest – would enter the Most Holy Place, and then only once a year, "and not without taking blood, which he offers for himself and for the unintentional sins of the people" (v. 7). The author of Hebrews teaches about this earthly holy place – the tabernacle – where people met God under the old covenant. However, with the incarnation and Jesus' inauguration of the new covenant, God dwells directly with his people in Christ Jesus himself.

> But when Christ appeared as a high priest of the good things that have come, then through the greater and more perfect tent (not made with hands, that is, not of this creation) he entered once for all into the holy places, not by means of the blood of goats and calves but by means of his own blood, thus securing eternal redemption. (vv. 11-12)

The author of Hebrews is here showing the Old Testament shadow and the New Testament fulfillment. God dwelt in the Most Holy Place in the tabernacle, but now dwells in the Person of Jesus Christ, *Emmanuel*, God with us.

The Old Testament Tabernacle was the temporary and portable place of worship of the Israelites until they had come into the promised land and were able to set up their permanent Temple in Jerusalem. But the structure of the Temple was similar, with a Most Holy Place or Holy of Holies where the presence of God rested and the high priest would enter for the atonement of sins. It is into this Temple that Mary, according to the *Protoevangelion*, is presented. One can clearly, then, see the relevance of such an epistle reading on this feast, for it describes the Temple worship as it was at the time of Mary's childhood.

However, there is another layer to the typological meaning of this feast and that is Mary as "Tabernacle," "Holy of Holies" and "Ark." The stichera at small vespers of the feast proclaim, "Into the holy places the Holy of Holies is fittingly brought to dwell."[100] She is called a "spotless Tabernacle of God the Almighty,"[101] "in truth the most holy Temple of our Holy God," and "the living Ark, that contained the Word who cannot be contained."[102] More will be said about this typology in a later chapter.

THE ANNUNCIATION OF THE THEOTOKOS

The epistle read at both the Annunciation and the Synaxis, Hebrews 2.11-18, as might be expected, has an incarnational theme. The author explains that Jesus and his followers "all have one origin. That is why he is not ashamed to call them brothers" (v. 11). In the incarnation Jesus took on human nature in order to redeem it. "He had to be made like his brothers in every respect, so that he might become a merciful and faithful high priest in the service of God, to make propitiation for the sins of the people. For because he himself has suffered when tempted, he is able to

---

[100] Mother Mary and Ware, 164.
[101] Ibid., 165
[102] Ibid., 166

help those who are being tempted" (vv. 17-18). St. John Chrysostom comments:

> He that is so great...was willing and earnest to become our sibling in all things, and for this cause did he leave the angels and the other powers and come down to us; he took hold of us and wrought innumerable things. He destroyed death, he cast out the devil from his tyranny, he freed us from bondage....[H]e took on himself our flesh, only for love to humankind, that he might have mercy upon us.[103]

The Annunciation (which is a feast of the Incarnation[104]) and the Synaxis of the *Theotokos* (which is a commemoration of the Virgin's role in the Incarnation) thus both point to the reality of God made flesh. That two such feasts are on the Christian calendar (and that the hymnody of other marian feasts constantly references Mary's birth-giving), makes central the fact that the driving force behind the veneration of the Mother of God is her role in the Incarnation.

The gospel of the feast, as might be expected, is the biblical narrative of the Annunciation, Luke 1.24-38. The structure of the narrative – including the pattern of birth announcements and the parallels to other annunciations – has been discussed in Chapter Two, as has the narrative context of the pericope. Only this feast and the Synaxis of the *Theotokos* have the benefit of being directly and explicitly Scriptural and so lend themselves to having their gospel tell the story of the commemoration. In this case, the gospel's inclusion is self explanatory.

---

[103] John Chrysostom, *On the Epistle to the Hebrews* 5.1-2, quoted in *Ancient Christian Commentary on Scripture: New Testament X: Hebrews* (Downers Grove, IL: InterVarsity Press, 2005), 49.

[104] "It is sometimes disputed whether the feast belongs primarily to the Mother of God or to our Lord, whose incarnation it celebrates. It both marks the beginning of our Savior's human life and, at the same time, is surely the greatest day in the life of Mary. In the Byzantine rite, however, the feast of the Annunciation belongs to The Blessed Virgin Mary, and the liturgy centers almost exclusively on the Mother of God." Shereghy, 92. Of course, any feast of the Mother of God is, ultimately, a feast of the Lord, because she gets her meaning entirely from him.

THE SYNAXIS OF THE THEOTOKOS

We turn finally to the Synaxis of the *Theotokos*, the feast of the Mother of God attached to the Nativity of our Lord. The epistle is the same as that of the Annunciation. The gospel, Matthew 2.13-23, picks up where the Christmas Liturgy left off (Matthew 2.1-2). Christmas Day's gospel lesson tells the story of the visit of the Magi to Bethlehem. The lesson on the Synaxis describes the holy family's flight into Egypt (vv. 13-15), the massacre of the innocents in Bethlehem (vv. 16-18), and the family's return to Nazareth (vv. 19-23).

Joseph is warned in a dream that they must leave Bethlehem for Egypt because Herod seeks to kill the Christ Child. In Egypt, Joseph is told, again in a dream, that it is safe to return to Nazareth. The Virgin does not figure prominently in this pericope. She is explicitly mentioned only twice, in verses 13 and 20, where Joseph is told to "Rise, take the child and his mother and" go to either Egypt or the land of Israel. This pericope, then, seems to be a continuation of the Christmas narrative that was begun with the liturgies on the preceding day. As discussed in Chapter Two, the Synaxis is more a continuation of the feast of the Lord's Nativity than it is a separate, stand-alone feast. The proper epistle and gospel lessons seem to confirm this.

Chapter Four
Extra-Biblical Feasts of the Theotokos

The major events in the life of the Lord are observed liturgically throughout the year – his conception (Annunciation, 25 March), birth (25 December), Presentation (2 February), death (Holy and Great Friday) and resurrection (Pascha). Christ, as the new Adam and the "firstfruits" of humanity to be raised up, has given all of humanity the opportunity to be made like him, conformed to his image, and ultimately brought to glorification through him.[105] The Church teaches that, among non-divine humanity, the Mother of God is the first to be granted this glory. And so it is logical that the church should also celebrate her life in a comparable format. The Virgin's conception, birth, entrance into the Temple, and death are all observed ritually as a sort of 'shadow' or reflection of the life of Jesus Christ, whom she served with humility.

The canonical scriptures, however, while giving us the details of the major points in the life of Christ, refrain from giving much detail about the *Theotokos* at all, and certainly not these points in her life. For the content of these, the Church has turned to other ancient and venerable texts and traditions which, while not being of the same canonical value, still point the faithful to truths of the mystery of our faith. We now turn to the four major non-biblical feasts of the *Theotokos*.

THE CONCEPTION OF THE THEOTOKOS
BY THE HOLY ANNA

Not considered to be one of the Twelve Great Feasts, the Feast of the Conception of the *Theotokos* by the Holy Anna (or, alternatively, the Maternity of Holy Anna) is celebrated by the Churches of the Byzantine East on 9 December, one day less than

---

[105] See 1 Corinthians 15.

nine months before the celebration of the Virgin's birth.[106] In Byzantine thought, females were in the womb one day less than males. The earliest extant record of this feast is in the typicon of St. Sabbas, dating from the late 5th century, in which it is entitled "The Conception of St. Anna."[107] Shereghy notes that this typicon is itself a revision of an earlier typicon. However whether or not this feast was included in the earlier one is a matter of speculation. He argues, however, that the feast must be a bit earlier than the typicon, on the basis of parallels with the life of Christ and that of the Forerunner.

> The feast of the Conception of the Mother of God is similar in its basic idea to the conceptions of Christ and of John the Baptist as described in Sacred Scripture. The child-begetting of St. Elizabeth, mother of John the Baptist, was celebrated both in East and West as was the conception of Christ, the Annunciation. By virtue of this analogy, we may deduce that the Conception of the Mother of God must have been celebrated about the same time, that is, in the fifth century.[108]

At least from the eighth century, it was observed on 9 December.[109] Graef considers that it was, at this time, a fairly recent addition to Byzantine liturgical spirituality.[110] In a sermon by John of Eubea (d. 750), the feast is commemorated, though he notes that the feast "is not known by all."[111]

The content of this feast largely draws upon a mid-second to early-third-century apocryphal text, the *Protoevangelium*, so-called, attributed to St. James, the kinsman of the Lord. While

---

[106] The Byzantine Ruthenian Metropolitan Church of Pittsburgh observes this feast on 8 December, following Western practice. This is because the Catholic Church has placed the United States under the patronage of the Immaculate Conception. The Ruthenians, therefore, celebrate their feast in solidarity with the Roman Rite's commemoration of the Immaculate Conception.
[107] Katrij, Julian J., OSBM, *A Byzantine Rite Liturgical Year*. (New York: Basilian Fathers Publication, 1983), 275; Shereghy, 66.
[108] Ibid., 67
[109] Calabuig, 284.
[110] Graef, 141-142.
[111] Calabuig, 284-285, n. 285.

much of this text alludes to the canonical gospels, the annunciation narrative for the conception of Mary does not follow the biblical precedent. Joachim and Anna had been barred from offering their sacrifices at the Temple, the priest Reuben taking their barrenness as a sign of God's displeasure with them (1.2)[112]. Joachim, being a righteous man, goes out into the wilderness to fast until the Lord visits him with an explanation (1.4). While he is gone, Anna sings a lamentation in which she recognizes that she is not even as blessed as the birds, dumb animals, beasts of the earth, or waters, for all of these things are fruitful (3.1-3). At the end of her lament, "an angel of the Lord" comes to her and announces

> "Anna, Anna, the Lord has heard your prayer. You shall conceive and bear and your offspring shall be spoken of in the whole world". And Anna said: "As the Lord my God lives, if I bear a child, whether male or female, I will bring it as a gift to the Lord my God, and it shall serve him all the days of its life". (4.1)

Whereas, as discussed in chapter two, biblical annunciations include the five-fold pattern of *appearance, fear, message, objection,* and *sign*, the annunciation to Saint Anna is much more straightforward: *appearance* and *message*. Anna does not show any fear, nor make any objection, nor need a sign to reassure her. Joachim, evidently, at the same time is visited by an angel who also tells him that Anna will conceive (4.2).

Although it does not follow the biblical pattern textually, it does follow the canonical precedent of righteous people, formerly childless, finally receiving the blessing of a child. This is the case with Isaac, Samson, John the Forerunner, and Jesus himself. In each case, the child of a formerly barren couple plays a significant role in the narrative.

The liturgical texts for this feast, as would be expected, draw upon the filling of a formerly barren womb. "Today the

---

[112] Throughout, the references to the *Protoevangelion* are from Edgar Hennecke, *New Testament Apocrypha (Vol. 1)*, Wilhelm Schneemelcher, ed. (Philadelphia: Westminster, 1963).

bonds of barrenness are loosed, for God has heard the prayers of Joachim and Anna. He promised, beyond hope, the birth of their godly daughter," proclaims the troparion. And the kontakion announces: "Today the world celebrates how Anna becomes a mother by the power of God. She conceived the woman whose conception of the Word is beyond our words."[113]

While extensive dogmatic discussion is beyond the scope of this present work, a word or two should be given regarding the "Immaculate Conception" of the Virgin Mary. On 8 December 1854, Pope Pius IX, in the apostolic constitution *Ineffabilis Deus* promulgated the following definition of the dogma of the Immaculate Conception:

> We declare, pronounce, and define that the doctrine which holds that the most Blessed Virgin Mary, in the first instance of her conception, by a singular grace and privilege granted by Almighty God, in view of the merits of Jesus Christ, the Savior of the human race, was preserved free from all stain of original sin, is a doctrine revealed by God and therefore to be believed firmly and constantly by all the faithful.[114]

Jaroslav Pelikan (at the time a Lutheran, later an Orthodox Christian), in his discussion of the dogma, rightly points out that, while much of marian doctrine appeared first in the Christian East and was later adopted by the West, the historical development of this particular doctrine "was in great measure confined to the Latin West."[115] This is because, in large part, the idea of a "stain" of original sin, is an idea foreign to the Eastern theological mind. Meyendorff explains:

> Byzantine homiletic and hymnographical texts often praise the Virgin as "fully prepared," "cleansed," and "sanctified." But these texts are to be understood in the

---

[113] *The Divine Liturgies of Our Holy Fathers John Chrysostom and Basil the Great* (Pittsburgh: Byzantine Catholic Metropolitan Church *Sui Juris* of Pittsburgh, USA, 2006), 277-278.
[114] *Ineffabilis Deus*, online at: http://www.papalencyclicals.net/Pius09/p9ineff.htm
[115] Pelikan, 189.

context of the doctrine of original sin which prevailed in the East: the inheritance from Adam is mortality, not guilt, and there was never any doubt among Byzantine theologians that Mary was indeed a *mortal* being.[116]

Both Catholics and Orthodox agree that the *Theotokos* was free from *actual* sin. The controversy is whether or not she was free from *original* sin. The answer to this question, then, varies because of the different ways in which original sin is understood. Metropolitan Kallistos explains the points on which Greek East and Latin West can agree:

> The consequences of Adam's disobedience extended to all his descendents. We are members of one another, as St Paul never ceased to insist, and if one member suffers the whole body suffers. In virtue of this mysterious unity of the human race, not only Adam but all humankind became subject to mortality. Nor was the disintegration which followed from the fall merely physical. Cut off from God, Adam and his descendants passed under the domination of sin and of the devil. Each new human being is born into a world where sin prevails everywhere, a world in which it is easy to do evil and hard to do good. Our will is weakened and enfeebled by what Greeks call 'desire' and the Latins call 'concupiscence.' We are all subject to these, the spiritual effects of sin.[117]

However, while Latin and Greek agree on these points, the Orthodox do not believe that actual sin is now a *necessity* for one under original sin. "They cannot," writes Kallistos, "agree with Augustine, when he writes that humans are under 'a harsh necessity' of committing sin, and that 'human nature was overcome by the fault into which it fell, *and so came to lack freedom.*'"[118] Moreover, because the East is universal in its acceptance of the real, physical death of the Mother of God, and

---

[116] Meyendorff, 147.
[117] Ware, *Orthodox Church*, 223.
[118] Ibid.

because death was introduced into the world by original sin, it becomes hard for them to say that the Virgin was without original sin.[119]

However, the issue is, perhaps, not as clear cut as all of this. The Orthodox object to the dogma because original sin, they say, is the inheritance of mortality and concupiscence/desire. They object to the idea of inherited guilt. However, the Roman Church is careful to nuance its understanding of original sin.[120] "Although it is proper to each individual, original sin does not have the character of a personal *fault* in any of Adam's descendants. It is a deprivation of original holiness and justice, but human nature has not been totally corrupted: it is wounded in the natural powers proper to it; subject to ignorance, suffering, and the dominion of death; and inclined to sin…"[121] What is curious is that original sin is not dogmatized in such a way as to understand original sin as a "stain," but yet the dogma of the Immaculate Conception speaks of Mary's freedom from the "stain of original sin."

On the other side of the argument, the Latins can point to some precedent in the East for their understanding that Mary was "immaculately" conceived. Saint John of Damascus explicitly refers to it. "For John, both the Virgin Mary's conception and her birth took place completely under the influence of divine grace."[122] And they can point to the many instances when the Eastern Churches refer to Mary, liturgically, as "immaculate" or "without stain" (Gr. *panamomos*) and "spotless" (Gr. *achrantos*).

For the Orthodox, such a dogma is seen as, in the first place, an unnecessary show of papal power and, in the second place, *"an incorrect expression of a correct idea about the personal sinlessness of the Mother of God."*[123]

---

[119] To further complicate matters, there is not a consensus on the matter even among Eastern theologians. While most did not accept the same understanding of "original sin" as Western theologians, some were quite strong on the point, e.g. Gregory the Theologian.

[120] Admittedly, Roman theology on the matter was less nuanced in the 19th century, when the dogma of the Immaculate Conception was defined.

[121] *Catechism of the Catholic Church*, 2nd ed., 405 (emphasis added)

[122] Gambero, 402.

[123] Sergius Bulgokov, *The Burning Bush: On the Orthodox Veneration of the Mother of God* (Grand Rapids, MI: Eerdmans, 2009), 48, emphasis in the original.

It is unlikely that this disagreement between Latin and Greek Christianity will be settled in any definitive way soon.[124] And the scope and intention of the present work does not allow for a full treatment of it. At the very least we can say a few things: Catholics and Orthodox agree that Mary was without actual sin, was prepared uniquely to be the *Theotokos*, and that she is the most complete example of a human being submitting to the will of the Almighty. Bulgakov writes:

> The Mother of God by the power of her personal freedom and the grace of the Holy Spirit is completely free of every personal sin during and after her birth. Therefore, original sin has power in her only as an infirmity of human nature, but it is deprived of its seductiveness and is powerless to summon sinfulness even as an imagined assault of sin or an involuntary movement of lust. Such is the understanding of this question in Orthodox doctrine...[125]

At the end of the day, the dogma makes little liturgical difference, even among those Eastern Christians in union with Rome. The overwhelming theme of the feast is the removal of Saint Anna's barrenness. The Byzantine Catholic Church, while in America it has moved the date of the feast to coincide with the Latin observance of the Immaculate Conception, does not itself celebrate the Immaculate Conception, but the older feast, the Maternity of Saint Anna. And the hymns sung for the feast are the same as those of the Orthodox East.[126]

---

[124] While the author of this present work is no expert in dogmatic theology, it seems that with a nuanced understanding of original sin, the dogma of the Immaculate Conception could be accepted by a Christian of the Byzantine tradition without any damage done to the ancient and venerable theological heritage of that Church. It need not be a Church-dividing issue.

[125] Bulgakov, 44-45

[126] It is true that in some places, through processes of Latinization, the feast was entitled "The Immaculate Conception of the Most Holy Mother of God" (see, for instance, Shereghy, 66) and that the hymnody was modified to emphasize Mary's "immaculate" status. However, with the Second Vatican Council and recent Popes urging the Eastern Catholics to return to their "ancient and venerable" traditions, these Latinizations have been and are being undone.

THE NATIVITY OF OUR
MOST HOLY LADY THE THEOTOKOS

Nine months after the observance of the Virgin's conception, the Church celebrates her birth, the first of the twelve great feasts to be celebrated in the liturgical year. Whether this feast predates that of her conception or not is unknown. Bradshaw and Johnson connect this feast to an early church in Jerusalem which was dedicated to the Mother of God[127]. This church, next to Pool of Bethesda,[128] was near to Saint Anna's home and, therefore, considered to be the place of Mary's birth.[129] Calabuig identifies the year of its dedication "toward the end of the fifth century."[130] Bradshaw and Johnson suggest a later date of 543.[131] They give two possible explanations for the connection of the dedication of this church to the feast of the Virgin's birth.

> ...The annual anniversary of this dedication may be the origins of the feast, the thematic contents of which were supplied by the *Protoevangelium of James*. While this explanation is probable, the mere fact that the church was built on this site may suggest, alternatively, that there was already a commemoration of Mary's birth on 8 September in Jerusalem at this site that gave rise both to the feast and to the dedication of the church on this date, rather than the other way around.[132]

That Saint Anna's home was near the Pool of Bethesda may be coincidental or there may have been a practical reason. Calabuig argues, following E. Testa, that, "Anna, seeking to be healed

---

[127] Adolf Adam identifies this church as being "St. Anne's," rather than the Virgin's. *The Liturgical Year: It's History & It's Meaning After the Reform of the Liturgy.* (NY: Pueblo Publishing Company, 1981), 217.

[128] See John 5.1-15

[129] Bradshaw and Johnson, 211.

[130] Calabuig, 254.

[131] Bradshaw and Johnson, 211.

[132] Ibid., 211-212

from her infertility, used the healing waters of the shrine. Testa, in fact, sees in chapters 1-4 of the *Protoevangelium of James* traces of the 'healing ritual' used in the pool."[133]

The narrative content of the feast comes from a very small pericope of the *Protoevangelium*.

> And her six months [her months] were fulfilled, as (the angel) had said: in the seventh [ninth] month Anna brought forth. And she said to the midwife: "What have I brought forth?" And she said: "A female". And Anna said: "My soul is magnified this day". And she lay down. And when the days were fulfilled, Anna purified herself from her childbed and gave suck to the child, and called her Mary. (5.2)

From this short passage the hymns of the feast expand into a multifold layered celebration of the Virgin's birthday. Additional words are given to Anna: "'O Lord, Thou hast hearkened to my prayer,' let Ann exclaim. 'Thou hast granted me today the fruit of the promise, her that among all generations and woman was foreordained to be Thy pure and undefiled Mother.'"[134] And the *Protoevangelium* is directly referred to by Romanus the Melodist: "The prayer and groaning of Joachim and Ann at their barrenness and childlessness have proved acceptable, and have come unto the ears of the Lord... The one offered his prayer in the mountain, the other bore her reproach in the garden."[135] Throughout the hymns, the theme of Anna's barrenness being overthrown is prevalent.

Within these hymns, Mary's role as a connection or bridge between the Old Testament and the New Testament is emphasized. She is repeatedly hymned as the "rod" or "branch" of Jesse, out of which the "flower" will come. Isaiah states, "There shall come forth a rod from the root of Jesse, and a flower shall grow out of this root." (Is. 11.1) In these hymns the Virgin is seen as the "rod" and Christ, her offspring, as the "flower."

---

[133] Calabuig, 254.
[134] Mother Mary and Kallistos, 115.
[135] Ibid., 119

"From Ann today," state the stichera at Vespers, "has sprung forth a rod, a branch given by God, even the *Theotokos*, salvation of men."[136] At Matins of the feast, in the second canon on Canticle Three, this flowering branch is connected further to the wood of the Cross (the Exaltation of which is celebrated just five days later): "The rod of Aaron is an image of this mystery, for when it budded it showed who should be priest. So in the Church, that once was barren, the wood of the Cross has now put forth flower, filling her with strength and steadfastness."[137] This Old Testament/New Testament connection is further explored through other typology: Anna is likened to Sarah, who had formerly been barren[138] and Mary is called "Tabernacle and Gate, spiritual Mountain, Bush and Rod of Aaron sprung from the root of David."[139]

Mary's role as the "new Eve" is also made apparent at Vespers of the feast. "She is the divine sanctuary of the eternal Essence; through her cruel hell has been trampled under foot, and Eve with all her line is established secure in life."[140] "Let Adam our forefather be glad and let Eve rejoice with great joy. For behold, she who was made from the rib of Adam plainly declares her daughter and descendant blessed."[141]

> What is this sound of feasting that we hear? Joachim and Ann mystically keep festival. 'O Adam and Eve', they cry, 'rejoice with us today: for if by your transgression ye closed the gate of Paradise to those of old, we have now been given a glorious fruit, Mary the Child of God, who opens its entrance to us all.'[142]

Mary is seen as the "temple" or "tabernacle" of God throughout the feast, emphasizing her role as the God-bearer.

---

[136] Ibid., 98.
[137] Ibid., 113.
[138] Ibid., 114.
[139] Ibid., 115.
[140] Ibid., 105.
[141] Ibid., 104.
[142] Ibid., 105.

She is called "habitation of God" and "divine sanctuary;"[143] God's "holy throne upon earth" and "a living heaven;"[144] the "Holy of Holies;"[145] the "living Temple of God," "a heaven and throne of God," and "the living Pavilion of His divine glory"[146] and "the preordained tabernacle of our reconciliation with God."[147] This is a theme that is taken up and further developed in the feast of her Entrance into the Temple.

Like all of the feasts of the Virgin, everything we say about Mary is seen in light of her Son. The emphasis is always on Mary as Virgin Mother of the Word of God incarnate. It is an intensely Christological feast. The birth of the Mother of God is, obviously, an important step in the human side of the process which culminates in the birth in the flesh of our Lord. This emphasis on the incarnational (and thus Christological) aspect of the feast can be seen in the troparion of the feast.

> Your birth, O Virgin *Theotokos*, heralded joy to the universe; for from you arose the Sun of Justice, Christ our God. Removing the curse, he gave the blessing, and by destroying death, he granted us eternal life.[148]

In other words, the birth in holiness of the *Theotokos* is celebrated precisely *because* it is part of the life-giving and restorative work of God among mortals. Mary, in her humility, is simply an "instrument" in the incarnation, that "marvelous mystery of the ineffable union of the natures which come together in Christ. Worshipping *Him*, we sing the praises of the all-spotless birth of the Virgin."[149] Her role as the bearer of the

---

[143] Ibid., 105
[144] Ibid., 100.
[145] Ibid., 111.
[146] Ibid., 106.
[147] Ibid., 121
[148] *The Divine Liturgies of Our Holy fathers John Chrysostom and Basil the Great*, 243. Note the similarities to the troparion of Christmas: "Your birth, O Christ our God, has shed upon the world the light of knowledge; for through it, those who worshipped the stars have learned from a star to worship you, the Sun of Justice, and to know you, the Dawn from on High. Glory to you, O Lord!" *The Divine Liturgies of Our Holy fathers John Chrysostom and Basil the Great*, 290.
[149] Mother Mary and Kallistos, 121, emphasis added.

Son of God is never far from the minds of those who keep this holy day.

THE ENTRANCE OF THE MOST HOLY THEOTOKOS INTO THE TEMPLE

The third feast of the *Theotokos* which borrows its content from the *Protoevangelium* is the Entrance of the Most Holy *Theotokos* Into the Temple, also sometimes called the "Presentation" or "Introduction" of the Mother of God.[150] This feast, like that of Mary's nativity, seems to have originally been a local festival associated with the dedication of a church in Jerusalem, "the Nea or New church, dedicated on 21 November 543."[151] If the commemoration were to follow the *Protoevangelium's* narratively closely, of course, it would be celebrated on the same day as Mary's birth, for the events commemorated are recorded as having taken place on her third birthday. Shereghy indicates that this celebration, "at least in a symbolic sense" was as early as the fourth century, but he gives no specific evidence for this claim.[152] Thomas Hopko cites Vladimir Lossky as noting that St. Andrew of Crete knew of its celebration in Jerusalem in the seventh century.[153] It was being celebrated in the Great Church of Constantinople by the eighth century.[154]

The narrative content of the feast is, like that of the nativity of Mary, a very short pericope: in this case, only three verses long.

And when the child was three years old, Joachim said: "Let us call the undefiled daughters of the Hebrews, and let each one take a lamp, and let these be burning, in order

---

[150] Shereghy, 62.

[151] Bradshaw and Johnson, 212. See also Adam, 221.

[152] Shereghy, 63.

[153] Thomas Hopko, *Speaking the Truth in Love: The Entrance of the Theotokos Into the Temple.* (20 November 2009). Online: http://ancientfaith.com/podcasts/hopko/the_entrance_of_the_*theotokos*_into_the_templ e. Retrieved 23 October 2011.

[154] Adam, 221.

that the child may not turn back and her heart be enticed away from the temple of the Lord." And he did so until they went up to the temple of the Lord. And the priest took her and kissed her and blessed her, saying: "The Lord has magnified your name among all generations; because of you the Lord at the end of the days will manifest his redemption to the children of Israel." And he placed her on the third step of the altar, and the Lord God put grace upon the child, and she danced for joy with her feet, and *the whole house of Israel loved her*. And her parents went down wondering, praising and glorifying the almighty God because the child did not *turn back* [to them]. And Mary was in the temple nurtured like a dove and received food from the hand of an angel. (7.2-8.1)

The story is further elaborated in some places (not within the *Protoevangelium* itself) that the child Mary even "sat within the Holy of Holies in the Temple"[155] and was raised by "temple virgins."[156]

Of course, this, like the other feasts drawn from the *Protoevangelium* is not literally and historically true. This apocryphal work (which will be looked at briefly in the next chapter) was not written with a concern for historicity in the modern sense. Rather, this story is

a theological, poetical, mystical, liturgical contemplation that lived within the living, oral tradition of the Church, and by the sixth century was put together into a liturgical celebration for the edification of the faithful in order to make very firm, clear and absolutely true doctrinal dogmatic affirmations, teachings. In other words, it's made to contemplate the truth of the Christian faith."[157]

It is not feasible that the Temple hierarchy of the First Century BCE would have permitted anyone other than the high priest –

---

[155] Hopko. See, e.g., the Aposticha at Small Vespers of the Feast.
[156] Adam, 221.
[157] Hopko.

much less a girl – to enter the holy places of the Temple. And there is no scriptural or historical warrant for a class of "temple virgins" in the Jewish tradition.

Nonetheless the church, particularly in the East, felt that this feast proclaimed an important reality about the person of the *Theotokos* and, by extension, an important truth about Christians in general. It, like the feast of Mary's birth, continues the emphasis on Mary as the bridge between the old and new covenants. It further celebrates the preparation of Mary to be the *Theotokos*. "Mary is in the Temple, Israel's holiest place, because, having conceived the Son of God within her womb, she is herself the holy temple of the Most High."[158]

The festal hymns expand the narrative found in the *Protoevangelium*. The high priest is identified as Zechariah, father of John the Baptist, and the angel who fed Mary is identified as the Archangel Gabriel. Words are put in the characters' mouths: Anna exclaims, "O Zacharias, take her whom the prophets of God proclaimed in the Spirit, and lead her into the holy temple, there to be brought up in reverence, that she may become the divine Throne of the Master of all, His Palace, His resting-place, and His dwelling filled with light."[159] Likewise, Zachariah says to the Virgin, "O Gate of the Lord! Unto thee I open the gates of the temple: rejoice and go round it in gladness."[160] In allusion to Old Testament sacrificial law, Mary is likened to an offering and sacrifice in the Temple: Joachim and Anna "have offered unto God, as a three year old victim of sacrifice, the Queen without blemish,"[161] "holy and utterly without spot."[162]

One emphasis of the feast day hymns is the preparation Mary receives in the Temple to become the Mother of God. "Thou art dedicated in the temple of God," the *irmos* of Canticle One declares, "to be prepared as a divine dwelling place for His coming."

---

[158] Calabuig, 296.
[159] Mother Mary and Kallistos, 167.
[160] Ibid., 171.
[161] Ibid., 170.
[162] Ibid., 177.

But the strongest emphasis (which is hinted at already in some of Mary's other feasts) is, to use Bulgakov's term, her "templification." On this day the parallels between the Tabernacle and Temple of the Old Testament and Mary herself in the New Testament are made most obvious. Mary is the Temple admitted to the Temple, the Holy of Holies who dwells in the Holy of Holies. She is the Tabernacle (literally "dwelling-place") of God himself, in the person of Jesus Christ. "O venerable Holy of Holies," the second canon at Matins says, "thou dost love to dwell in the holy temple."[163] Of this feast, Bulgakov writes:

> The entrance into the temple of the living Temple of God, the templification of the Virgin Mary, corresponds to the next step in the sanctification of the Mother of God. The temple was the only place on earth hallowed in peace where God lived.... This was the place of paradise in the earth of the curse, which here was removed from the world and creation, for the temple was holy. In this holy place, where angels would descend, the Most Holy Virgin was brought into communion with them, led into the Holy of Holies by the High Priest, in accordance with prophetic inspiration. Since that time the power of the Old Testament Temple already begins to be abolished as the sole place of encounter of humankind with God. Mary becomes the temple of the temple, and receives on herself the power of the temple's consecration. The significance of the temple is already exhausted, and it is left to be but a place of prayerful encounter until that moment when the curtain will be torn asunder and the Old Testament temple sanctuary abolished.[164]

The inclusion of the Epistle to the Hebrews makes this connection more apparent. In that epistle (though not in the pericope read at the Divine Liturgy) Jesus is explained to be the *tabernacling*, i.e. dwelling, of God among humanity. Here, because Mary's womb itself will be the dwelling place of God-in-

---

[163] Ibid., 180.
[164] Bulgakov, 66.

the-Flesh, she is the temple, the palace, the tabernacle and the bridal chamber of the Most High; she is the Holy of Holies.

This "templification," in turn, has further implications for all who would be disciples of Jesus. In this, Mary becomes the model and archetype for all Christians. "What is being contemplated in the person of Mary as the central character in the story is that human beings are created by God and redeemed by God in Christ and sanctified by God through Christ by the Holy Spirit to become *living temples of God himself.*"[165] Mary is "the quintessential Christian."[166] What she is, we are called to be. What she has done, we are called to do. Under the new covenant, the dwelling place of God is not a temple in Jerusalem, but in the human heart. Mary exemplifies this, being full of grace. Her entrance into the temple, as Bulgakov explains, is the beginning of the end of the temple as the unique meeting place of humankind with God; it is "the fulfillment of the physical Temple and its ending."[167]

> This feast honoring Mary really points to Christ who fulfills the entire Old Testament, the Law and the Prophetic teachings. Christ is our High Priest, the one who makes the one complete and perfect sacrifice on the cross and who offers Himself for our salvation. Christ completes what the Old Testament priesthood could not do, provide the perfect sacrifice for the sins of the people. However, in order to bring about our salvation through Christ, God worked through Mary and her obedience which included her entrance into the Temple.[168]

THE DORMITION OF THE THEOTOKOS

The final marian feast with which we shall concern ourselves is that of the Dormition (i.e., "falling asleep") of our Most Holy Lady the *Theotokos* and Ever-Virgin Mary, to use its

---

[165] Hopko.
[166] Ibid.
[167] Ibid.
[168] William C. Mills, *Feasts of Faith: Reflections on the Major Feast Days.* (Rollinsford, NH: Orthodox Research Institute, 2008), 33.

full title. This commemorates the end of the earthly life of our Lady. Since most saints are commemorated on the anniversary of their deaths, this feast ought not to be particularly controversial. However, in the Western Church there was (and continues to be) some question over whether or not the Mother of God actually died before her Assumption.[169] Furthermore, although the East celebrates the feast of her death, the hymns of the feast very clearly point to believe in her bodily Assumption *after* death, which is a point of controversy with Protestants. So it turns out that it is a feast not without controversy at all. For the Christian East, however, there is no question of Mary's physical death, nor of her bodily assumption.[170] St. Andrew of Crete argued that Mary would not have escaped the experience of death since not even Jesus Christ himself avoided it. She was subject to mortality, but not because of any sin.

> Death, natural to men, also reached her; not, however, to imprison her, as happens to us, or to vanquish her. God forbid! It was only to secure for her the experience of that sleep which comes from on high, leading us up to the object of our hope.[171]

Whereas in Constantinople the earliest marian feast was that of the *Theotokos* connected with Christmas, in Jerusalem, 15 August was the earliest.[172] Rather than of historical origin, it is probably of geographical significance; that is, associated with a stational church in Jerusalem. Bradshaw and Johnson note that "the oldest Marian feast in existence is usually identified as the 15 August celebration of Mary *Theotokos*, having its origins in Jerusalem and first documented in the fifth-century Armenian Lectionary, one of our major guides to liturgical life in late-fourth-century Jerusalem."[173] This may have been assumed to be the day of her death. This seems to be the position of Adolf

---

[169] See, e.g., Pelikan, 208-209.
[170] Ware, *Church*, 260.
[171] St. Andrew of Crete, *Homily 1 on the Dormition*, PG 97, 1052 C-1053A, quoted in Gambero, 395.
[172] Fassler, 46.
[173] Bradshaw and Johnson, 206.

Adam.[174] However other explanations have been given: this may have been "the date of the Kathisma's dedication" or it may have been the case that the Jerusalem Church wanted to "distanc[e] itself from Constantinople's Christmas-related feast....But no one has been able to offer conclusive arguments beyond speculation as to why 15 August in particular became the date of this feast."[175] At any rate, the feast spread from Jerusalem to Byzantium by the late sixth century under the Emperor Maruice.[176] The Dormition of the Mother of God seems to have been celebrated at least as early as the fourth century.[177] In 496, Pope Gelasius considered the 15 August feast to be "very old."[178]

The narrative content of the feast is, as Basil Shereghy says, two-fold. It commemorates both the death of the *Theotokos* and her assumption into heaven. Neither of these events is found in Holy Scripture, but there are several apocryphal writings which tell the story in various ways. The Church – whether in the East or the West – has not approved any of these *transitus* (i.e. passing) stories as authoritative. Some stories place her death in Ephesus, others in Jerusalem.

One of the earliest of these narratives, *The Book of John Concerning the Falling Asleep of Mary*, falsely attributed to St. John the Theologian, is of the Jerusalem tradition. In it the Virgin Mother of God, who lives in Jerusalem, had a custom of regularly visiting the Holy Sepulchre of the Lord and saying prayers there. One day while visiting the tomb, the Archangel Gabriel appears to her and tells her that her prayers have been heard and that she will soon be reunited with her son. She rose and went to Bethlehem and prayed that the Apostle John would be brought to her with the other apostles. John, "just as [he] was going in to the holy altar in Ephesus to perform divine service," was "snatched up" in a "cloud of light" and spirited away to Jerusalem to the bed-side of the Virgin.[179] Soon thereafter Peter, Paul, and the

---

[174] Adam, 215.
[175] Bradshaw and Johnson, 207.
[176] Adam, 215.
[177] Bradshaw and Johnson, 206; Marion Hatchett, *Commentary on the American Prayer Book* (San Francisco: Harper, 1995), 71.
[178] Shereghy, 108.
[179] *The Book of John Concerning the Falling Asleep of Mary*, ANF, vol. 8, 587. 588.

other apostles are brought mysteriously to Jerusalem from various places throughout the world. Some of the apostles, who had already died, were raised up and brought there with the instruction from the Holy Spirit: "Do not think that it is now the resurrection; but on this account you have risen out of your tombs, that you may go to give greeting to the honour and wonder-working of the mother of our Lord and Saviour Jesus Christ, because the day of her departure is at hand, of her going up into the heavens."[180]

The religious elite among the Jews are enraged at the wonders occurring there in Bethlehem and desired to chase them out of Bethlehem, so the Holy Spirit instructs them to take the Virgin on her couch and they will be taken "by a cloud" to Jerusalem. The cloud takes them and deposits them in the Virgin's house. After five days of prayer and praise, the time for the Virgin's death was at hand, on a Sunday. She falls asleep in grace and the apostles carry her on a couch in procession. During the procession a "well-born Hebrew" named Jephonias touched the couch with both his hands. Her arms were severed and hung on the bier. This is reminiscent of the canonical story in 2 Kingdoms 6, regarding the ark of the covenant:

> And when they came to Nachon's threshing-floor, Uzzah placed his hand on the ark of God to hold it steady when the oxen shook it out of its place. The Lord was angered against Uzzah, and there God struck him. And before God, he died there next to the ark of the Lord. (2 Kingdoms 6.6-7)

This reiterates the ark-Mary connection that is so prevalent in Byzantine mariology. However, unlike Uzzah, Jephonias does not die. Instead, Peter declares: "thy hands which have been taken away from thee, will be fixed on again."[181] And his arms were re-attached.[182]

---

[180] Ibid., 588.
[181] Ibid., 591.
[182] Cf. Peter striking the soldier's ear and Christ re-attaching it in John 18.10-11; Luke 22.50-51.

In a "shadowing" of her son's death, Mary is laid in a "new tomb" and lies there for three days. During those three days "the voices of invisible angels were heard glorifying Christ our God, who had been born of her." When the voices stopped, the apostles knew that her body had been reunited with her soul in paradise.

This is, of course, a fanciful account and is not a matter of faith. Certainly the various "magical" events are not taken to be historically factual. However, that the Mother of God's body was "assumed" into paradise is certainly a matter of faith. For the Catholic Church, of course, it was decided definitively by Pope Pius XII's *Munificentissimus Deus* in 1950, which stated that "when the course of her earthly life was run, [Mary] was assumed in body and soul to heavenly glory." The Orthodox, while not dogmatizing the event, "firmly believes in [Mary's] Bodily Assumption."[183]

> Immediately after the Pope proclaimed the Assumption as a dogma in 1950, a few Orthodox (by way of reaction against the Roman Catholic Church) began to express doubts about the Bodily Assumption and even explicitly to deny it; but they are certainly *not* representative of the Orthodox Church as a whole.[184]

So the doctrine itself (if not the means of establishing it as dogma) is not a matter of division between Orthodox and Catholic. At any rate, liturgically speaking, both the Catholics of the Byzantine heritage and the Orthodox, share the same customs and hymnody for the feast, which is styled "the Dormition" and not "the Assumption."

Regardless of the fact that the pseudo-John's account of Mary's death is not taken to be historical, the imagery of the feast day hymns is largely drawn from this apocryphal text.[185] The story is re-told in poetic form, but significant pieces of the narrative remain intact. The disciples are somehow mystically

---

[183] Ware, *Church*, 260.
[184] Ibid., 260, n.1
[185] Mills, 108-109.

present at the event. "The honoured choir of the wise apostles was miraculously assembled," is sung at Matins; and at Vespers, "The assembly of the disciples is gathered together, come at an all-powerful behest from the ends of the earth..."[186]

In the liturgical witness, there is no question as to her physical, bodily death. The Apostles come "to bury the Mother and *Theotokos*."[187] They "surrounded [her] deathbed."[188]

> O pure Virgin, thou hast won the honor of victory over nature by bringing forth God; yet like thy Son and Creator, thou hast submitted to the laws of nature in a manner above nature. Therefore, dying thou hast risen to live eternally with thy Son.[189]

This shows, too, that her assumption, likewise, is extolled in the hymnody. "For the Virgin, the only *Theotokos*, is taken to her appointed dwelling-place in heaven."[190] "The earthly Heaven takes up her dwelling in a heavenly and imperishable land."[191]

Nor is it merely her soul which is taken to heaven, but her body as well. In this way, the feast might be said to be the resurrection of the *Theotokos*. At Matins, the first canon on Canticle Six confirms this in connecting Jonah's three days in the whale not only to the Resurrection of Christ (which is to be expected), but to Mary's assumption as well.

> For just as He kept thee virgin in thy childbirth so did He preserve thy body incorrupt in the tomb; and He glorified thee by a divine Translation, showing thee honour as a Son to His Mother.[192]

The Dormition of the Mother of God, then, is an eschatological sign. What has been done for Mary is what has

---

[186] Mother Mary and Ware, 512, 505.
[187] Ibid., 505.
[188] Ibid., 514.
[189] Ibid., 515.
[190] Ibid., 515.
[191] Ibid., 517.
[192] Ibid., 519.

been promised for all who are disciples of Jesus. Just as the holy Virgin serves as archetype for the believer in her submission to the will and workings of God in her life, thus making possible the Incarnation and thus the salvation of humankind, so her end is that of all who would be followers of the Cross. The connection of her being the God-bearer to her ultimate translation is made clear in the troparion of the feast:

> In giving birth, O *Theotokos*, thou hast retained thy virginity, and in falling asleep thou hast not forsaken the world. Thou who art the Mother of Life hast passed over into life, and by thy prayers thou dost deliver our souls from death.[193]

---

[193] Ibid., 511.

Chapter Five
A Brief Excursus on Narrative Texts

The modern person is concerned with historical fact: what is it, precisely and factually, that we can say about what has happened in the past? In biblical studies, this concern gave rise to the "Historical Jesus" movement and, more generally, to critical-historical inquiry into the Scriptures. When it comes to Mary the Virgin, we can say even less. The primary texts we turn to in order to discover who the *Theotokos* was are few: a small selection of mentions in the New Testament and several, much later, non-canonical writings. It is from these, together, perhaps, with the tradition of oral interpretation and embellishment, that the story of Mary's life comes down to us to the present day.

THE NEW TESTAMENT WITNESS

The earliest mention of Mary is in the New Testament, in St. Paul's Epistle to the Galatians (ca. 57 C.E.[194]), and even here, she is anonymous. "But when the fullness of time had come, God sent forth his Son, born of a woman," (4.4) writes the apostle. Later, as the writers of the gospels fleshed out the story of Jesus of Nazareth, they, too, mentioned his mother, but only as she is situated in *his* story.

In the Gospel of Matthew (ca 70 C.E.[195]) we learn about Jesus birth in 1.18-25. Mary is betrothed to Joseph, but they have not consummated the marriage. Joseph wants to "divorce her quietly" but Mary's virtue is confirmed by the apparition of an angel to him in a dream. Jesus is named by the angel in that dream. So Joseph accepts Mary as his wife but does not know

---

[194] See Marina Warner, *Alone of All Her Sex: The Myth and Cult of the Virgin Mary* (New York: Alfred Knopf, 1976), 3.
[195] David A. DeSilva, *An Introduction to the New Testament: Contexts, Methods & Ministry Formation* (Downers Grove, IL: InterVarsity Press, 2004), 238.

her "until she had given birth to a son" (v. 25).[196] Also in this gospel, the wise men come from "the east" and eventually find Jesus "with Mary his mother" (2.11). Because Herod is tipped off to a possibly messianic birth, the holy family is forced to flee to Egypt for safety. Joseph, warned in a dream, "rose and took the child and his mother by night and departed to Egypt" (2.14). After the slaughter of the Holy Innocents (2.16-18), Joseph, again has a dream, and brings Jesus and "his mother" back to Nazareth (2.19-23). She again appears in Matthew's gospel during Jesus' teaching ministry. While Jesus is preaching, "his mother and his brothers[197] stood outside, asking to speak with him" (12.46). Jesus seemingly dismisses them:

> But he replied to the man who told him, "Who is my mother and who are my brothers?" And stretching out his hand toward his disciples, he said, "Here are my mother and my brothers! For whoever does the will of my Father in heaven is my brother and sister and mother." (12.48-50)

In the Gospel According to Luke (after 70 C.E.[198]), Mary is more prominent simply because the Christmas narrative is more elaborate here. She appears, obviously, in the Annunciation narrative (1.26-38), in the Visitation to St. Elizabeth and sings the *Magnificat* (1.39-56). In the birth narrative of Jesus in chapter 2, we learn that Joseph and Mary have to go to Bethlehem to be "registered" by Roman law and it was here that she gave birth. Then we learn that shepherds, informed by an angel that the

---

[196] This "until," together with the phrase, "before they came together" in 1.18, has been a point of divergence in Catholic/Orthodox vs. Protestant interpretation. For the Protestant, this implies that Mary *did* eventually have intercourse with Joseph *after* the birth of Jesus. For the Catholic/Orthodox Christian, this interpretation flies in the face of the doctrine of Mary's perpetual virginity. For an *apologia* for the Catholic position, see Scott Hahn, *Hail Holy Queen: The Mother of God in the Word of God* (New York: Doubleday, 2001), 102-107.

[197] The word "brothers" here is, again, controversial. The semantic range of the word, however, includes "cousins," "relatives" or "kinsmen." Again, for a defense of the Catholic/Orthodox position, see Hahn, 102-107; or David Mills, *Discovering Mary: Answers to Questions About the Mother of God* (Cincinnati, OH: Servant Books, 2009), 24-26.

[198] See DeSilva, 308-309 for a discussion of the dating of Luke.

Christ child has been born, make their way into town where they "found Mary and Joseph, and the baby lying in a manger" (v. 16). When they explain how they had come to know about this, Mary "treasured up all these things, pondering them in her heart" (v. 19).

We also know from the Lukan gospel that Jesus was presented to be circumcised in the Temple (2.22-38). The righteous Simeon sang his *nunc dimittis* (vv. 29-32) and Jesus' "father and his mother marveled at what was said about him" (v. 33) Simeon then prophetically tells Mary,

> Behold, this child is appointed for the fall and rising of many in Israel, and for a sign that is opposed (and a sword will pierce through your own soul also), so that thoughts from many hearts may be revealed. (2.34-35)

The last appearance of Mary in Luke (2.41-51) is when the twelve-year-old Jesus is left at the Temple after their annual trip to Jerusalem to celebrate the Passover. After a day of traveling, they could not find him, so they returned to Jerusalem to look for him. "After three days they found him in the temple, sitting among the teachers, listening to them and asking them questions" (v. 46). His parents were "astonished."

> And his mother said to him, 'Son, why have you treated us so? Behold, your father and I have been searching for you in great distress.' And he said to them, 'Why were you looking for me? Did you not know that I must be in my Father's house? And they did not understand the saying that he spoke to them. And he went down with them and came to Nazareth and was submissive to them. And his mother treasured up all these things in her heart. (2.48-50)

In Luke 8.19-21, we have a pericope parallel to Matthew 12:46-50.

In the Gospel According to Mark (late 60s C.E.[199]), she appears, again with Jesus' "brothers" in a pericope that is parallel to Matthew 12.46-50 and Luke 8.19-21. Then she is mentioned again in Mark 6 when Jesus is rejected in his home town of Nazareth, when those who hear him ask, "Where did this man get these things? What is the wisdom given to him? How are such mighty works done by his hands? Is not this the carpenter, the son of Mary and brother of James and Joses and Judas and Simon? And are not his sisters here with us?" (6.2-3).

Mary appears twice in the Gospel According to John. First, at the "sign" at the wedding in Cana of Galilee (2.1-11).[200] Those who planned the wedding did not, evidently, plan for enough wine for all of the celebrants. Mary finds out and tells Jesus. Jesus replies, "Woman, what does this have to do with me? My hour has not yet come" (v.4). Mary, seemingly ignoring his objection, responds in a way that has great implications for a proper theological understanding of the role of the Mother of God. "His mother said to the servants, 'Do whatever he tells you'" (v. 5). She appears again in John 19 where she, together with the beloved disciple, are present for the crucifixion of Jesus.

> When Jesus saw his mother and the disciple whom he loved standing nearby, he said to his mother, "Woman, behold your son!" Then he said to the disciple, "Behold, your mother!" And from that hour the disciple took her to his own home (19.26-27).

Mary appears once in the Acts of the Apostles and once in the Apocalypse to John. In Acts we learn that, after the Ascension of Jesus, while they were waiting for the outpouring of the Holy Spirit at Pentecost, the apostles went to the "upper room, where they were staying" (v. 13). "All these [apostles] with one accord were devoting themselves to prayer, together

---

[199] For a brief discussion of the dating of the Gospel of Mark, see DeSilva, 196, 238.
[200] In the Typicon of the Great Church in Constantinople, there was a feast dedicated to Mary at Cana on the Monday following Thomas Sunday. As the Gospel of St. John was read in the Pentecostarion after Pascha, this feast was probably an elaboration on this pericope. See Juan Mateos, S.J., *Typicon de la Grande Église: Mss. (Timios Stauros 40)*. Rome: Pont. Institutum Orientalium Studiorum, 1962-3).

with the women and Mary the mother of Jesus, and his brothers" (v. 14). Presumably then, she is still present with them in chapter two, on the day of Pentecost. She is traditionally depicted as present in Byzantine icons of the feast.

In the Apocalypse, chapter 12, we find a "a woman clothed with the sun, with the moon under her feet, and on her head a crown of twelve stars. She was pregnant and was crying out in birth pains and the agony of giving birth" (vv. 1-2). A great, seven-headed dragon appears and attempts to snatch the child from her as she gives birth, so as to "devour" it. "She gave birth to a male child, one who is to rule all the nations with a rod of iron, but her child was caught up to God and to his throne" (v. 5). The woman then flees into "the wilderness" for 1,260 days (v. 6). Unlike the other New Testament mentions of the Mother of Jesus, however, this is not to be taken literally, as the vision in Revelation is one of spiritual or mystical truth.[201]

What are we to make of this New Testament witness? The New Testament is the only source for the life of Mary "with any claim to historical validity."[202] And it tells us precious little about her life. What they focus on is what is essential: her relationship to Jesus Christ. To look at *biblical* mariology is beyond the scope of this present work. However, the liturgical life of the Church is formed and influenced largely by these marian narratives. Certainly the feasts of the Annunciation and the Synaxis of the *Theotokos* are directly tied to Mary as found in the canonical gospels.

THE APOCRYPHAL WITNESS

The main apocryphal writings which bear on liturgical Mariology have both been briefly discussed in chapter four. The narrative content of the biblical canon is taken as true, more or

---

[201] Some scholars identify this woman not with the Mother of God, but with the Church. This would seem a bit of a stretch, for it is not the Church which gives birth to the Christ ("the one who is to rule all nations"). Rather, the Church gets its existence from Christ. However, as Mary is an icon and prototype of the Church and, in later theology, is identified as "Mother of the Church," perhaps this is one facet of the interpretation that bears examination.

[202] Warner, 3-4.

less at face value. Orthodox Christians do not question the historical reality of the Incarnation of the second Person of the Holy Trinity. The Annunciation and the Virgin Birth are accepted by Catholic, Orthodox and Protestant Christian alike.

The non-canonical or "apocryphal" texts present us with a different set of problems. Unlike the New Testament writings which were largely written before the end of the first century (and thus still within the memory of many of those who knew Jesus during his earthly ministry), the *Protoevangelium of James* and the *Book of John Concerning the Falling Asleep of Mary* originate much later.

Because the apostolic writings which found their way into our New Testament canon remained largely silent on the person of Mary herself, there began to be an "understandable and legitimate curiosity" concerning who she was. "In response to this need, the so-called New Testament *apocrypha* proliferated."[203] The historical, factual value of their narratives is negligible. However their historical value is, nonetheless, great, insofar as they show us how early marian piety began to be part of the life of the Church. They were not written to further expound central Christian tenets, but to "satisfy popular religious needs, and to promote beliefs about Mary which began to be held quite early on, although entirely without biblical foundation."[204] In attempting to answer the question of what is historical and what is legendary in apocryphal writings, Jacques Hervieux writes,

> Must we then ask whether we are dealing with history or legend? In reality, the nature of these works forbids our posing this question. For one reason, the ancients had no idea of purely objective history in the modern sense of the term. They did not simply relate the facts for their own sake: their "historical" literature was biassed [sic], it was intended to support a thesis. Furthermore, the East, where the kind of narration we call "popular history" had its origins, readily mixed legends with the events related, so

---

[203] Gambero, 33.
[204] Wybrew, 12.

that it is impossible to separate from the historical nucleus what is purely imaginary.[205]

The *Protoevangelium* is falsely attributed to James the Apostle, the brother of the Lord. In the 16th century, William Postel subtitled it "protoevangelium" or, "that which precedes the Gospel."[206] Wybrew dates it to the second half of the second century, Gambero to the middle of that century, and Hervieux places its origin earlier, from 130-140 C.E.[207] Gambero argues that, since the author seems to have little knowledge about Palestine or Jewish customs, the author was probably a non-Jew or, "at most, a Jew who lived outside of Palestine."[208] The *Protoevangelium* is certainly not canonical and was even condemned in a decree attributed to Pope Gelasius I (492-6). This attribution has been called into question in modern times, however, and the work has "been ascribed to an independent cleric of a century later, in southern Gaul or northern Italy, who did not have the authority of a pope to proscribe books."[209] Nonetheless, this prohibition did not stop Christians in both East and West – though primarily in the East[210] – from accepting the *Protoevangelium* on a non-canonical level. Indeed, the hymns for the feasts of Mary's conception, nativity and entrance into the temple, all rely on imagery from this text.

Mary's dormition and assumption are drawn from several *Transitus* (passing-over) accounts, one of the earliest of which is *The Book of John Concerning the Falling Asleep of Mary*, which has been discussed above. "All the eastern accounts – although they differ on the moment and manner of her death and translation into paradise – agree that the Virgin is passive, that her flesh at the moment of her glory is inert, if not inanimate."[211] In the Byzantine tradition, Mary truly dies (her "dormition") and

---

[205] Hervieux, 19.
[206] Ibid., 17.
[207] Wybrew, 11; Gambero, 35; Hervieux, 17.
[208] Gambero, 35.
[209] Warner, 29.
[210] Warner writes, "The east received the *Book of James* as authentic (it is extant in Greek, Ethiopic, and the oldest manuscript is in Syriac) but, surprisingly, it was not translated into Latin until the sixteenth century" (29-30).
[211] Warner, 84.

then is raised – one might say "resurrected" – body and soul and taken ("assumed") into heaven. While some Western authors questioned whether Mary truly died, there is no question of this in the East. Mary follows in the way of her Savior and Son: death, resurrection and ascension.

Marina Warner is critical of these *Transitus* accounts – not just their historicity, but also their literary value.

> Apart from the occasional scene of grandeur such as [the] moment of resurrection, the *Transitus* stories are poor literary speciments. Longwinded, puffed up, stuck in a morass of stock images and metaphysical formulas, the episodes are barren of spiritual content. The endless discourses of the apostles on their journey to Mary's bed, the disorganized and repetitive examples of the Jews' enmity: a sour mixture of credulity and prejudice characterizes the whole sequence. The Holy Ghost's magic itself is hardly awe-inspiring, but rather the cheap trickery of a child's conjuring kit...[212]

Nonetheless, as discussed above, the imagery from these accounts, especially that of the pseudo-John, is taken as the inspiration for the imagery in the poetry and prayer of the Byzantine rite regarding Mary's falling asleep. The important theological key to the feast, however, is that it concludes Mary's earthly life in a way promised to all believer's in Jesus: namely, that in the eschaton, we shall be raised to sit with God in glory everlasting.

---

[212] Ibid., 86.

Chapter Six
Toward a Byzantine Liturgical Mariology

We have now come to the end of this brief examination of selected marian feasts in the Byzantine rite. To what conclusion can we come? As we have looked over all six of these commemorations, each theme seems to point in one, unified direction, namely, the emphasis on Mary as Mother (or Bearer) of God, her role in the Incarnation in the flesh of our Lord and God and Savior Jesus Christ. Certainly the Annunciation to Mary and the Synaxis of the *Theotokos* (the two most ancient of our feasts) are explicitly connected to this reality. Being explicitly gospel feasts, and therefore being explicitly about Jesus Christ, the second Person of the Trinity, this connection is very clear. If Jesus is our Savior, then Mary's role in bringing him forth into the world is a central Christian matter of faith. "Mary's role in our salvation is deeply ingrained in the Church."[213]

As regards the non-biblical feasts of the *Theotokos*, this connection to her role in redemption may not be as clear, at least initially. However, if one looks at the theological and poetic themes that run throughout these feasts, it becomes obvious. The Maternity of Holy Anna and the Nativity of the *Theotokos* are concerned primarily with God's miraculous healing of Anna's barrenness. In this, the earthly family of Jesus is connected with the overarching salvation-history narrative of the Scriptures. Mary's birth is miraculous like those of the Patriarch Isaac, of the Prophet Samuel, and of the Forerunner John. Additionally, Mary's Nativity liturgically gives expression to the appearance of the "temple" of God – the first evidence that God's dwelling is no longer in the heavens and in the Holy of Holies in Jerusalem, but among (and indeed *within*) humankind. This theme is then taken up again, and expanded, in the Entrance of the *Theotokos* into the

---

[213] Mills, 3.

Temple. Mary enters the Temple in Jerusalem as a prefiguring of her becoming the Tabernacle (that is, the dwelling-place) of the Lord. It is the beginning of the end of the old covenant set-up. God, in the person of Jesus, first takes up dwelling in the womb of the Virgin to effect his Incarnation. Later, in part because of Mary's voluntary submission to the will of the Lord, God will take up residence in the hearts of all who repent and return to him. In Mary's becoming *Theotokos*, she becomes a model for all Christian people: the great example. For we, too, are called to bear God, not in the flesh, but in bringing him forth in our gospel words and deeds. She becomes the exemplar and model for all disciples of Jesus.

And if she is the model for us in her life, she becomes the example and foreshadowing of our future in her death. In her falling asleep, she undergoes precisely what the Scriptures promise for all those who love God, namely, the resurrection of the body, as we profess in our Creed.

So, while the Eastern Christian tradition says many of the same things that the Western tradition does regarding the Mother of God, she does not wander far from the first great dogmatic proclamation on Mary: that she is truly *Theotokos*. Regarding the Western approach to the Virgin, Archimandrite Robert Taft, SJ, writes,

> For centuries a sort of liturgical schitzophrenia was operative in Roman heortology, with new feasts instituted in total disregard of their integration into a coherent vision of the liturgical celebration of Salvation History. Thus Christ the King is celebrated in the autumn, when the obvious biblico-liturgical setting of that mystery is the triumphal entry into Jerusalem on Palm Sunday. And the month of May; in most years a Pentecostal season *par excellence*, is turned into the month of Mary, when a more obvious time for a "Marian month," as is clear in the Eastern Christian liturgical calendars, would be during the

Advent season, because of Mary's inseparable link with the mystery of the Incarnation.[214]

While this is not the context in which to evaluate the Western approach to the *Theotokos*, it may be safe to say that this liturgical and devotional development, which was very often done without regard to integrating it into the "biblico-liturgical" logic of salvation history, has led many to look to Mary in isolation from her role in the Incarnation – and therefore the salvation and glorification of humanity. While the East is not entirely blameless in this regard either, it's Mariological development and devotion tends to continue to center on Mary's connection with her Son and Savior. In the 20th Century the Catholic Church made its understanding of Mary an intentional area of its reform, bringing the Western approach more in line with the Eastern. Taft, in summarizing this approach (based upon *Lumen gentium* and *Sancrosanctum Concilium*) noted, among other things:

> The veneration of Mary, which has existed from the birth of the Church, is rooted in Scripture and Tradition, and based on her inseparable relationship to her Son in the History of Salvation....
>
> Veneration of Mary is not an absolute veneration of her as a separate individual, in isolation, based on personal qualities and merits unrelated to the gifts received from God. Rather, we venerate Mary for a holiness and a role in Salvation History that is totally relative and derived. It is inseparably related to her Divine Son's saving work, and derived and dependent on it. As Mary herself said, "All generations shall call me blessed" – but only "because he that is mighty hath done great things for me"

---

[214] Taft, "Marian Liturgical Veneration: Common Origins, Contemporary Catholic Renewal, and Meaning for Today," in *Orientale Lumen III Conference 1999 Proceedings*. June 15-18, 1999. Washington, DC., 104.

(Lk 1:48-49) – i.e., because of her role "in the mysteries of Christ."[215]

Mary, then, for the Eastern Christian, is venerated because she is the archetype and prototype of a Christian. Jesus is, of course, the perfect icon of God the Father – "He is the image of the invisible God" (Col. 1.15). He is the perfect man – and in his humanity has raised humanity. But Jesus is also perfect God. Mary, then, is the great example to us of what a redeemed human looks like. Her purity of life and her intercessions on our behalf find their origin and fulfillment in her humble and fruitful submission to the will of God, which resulted in her bringing forth God the Word in the flesh.

WHERE DO WE GO FROM HERE?

As was made clear from the outset of this study, we have not attempted to herein synthesize a complete and all-encompassing Mariology of the Byzantine tradition. We have simply looked at the foundation of the Eastern Christian life as it is lived out – namely, the liturgical life – to glean what we could of Byzantine Mariological beliefs from it.

In order to flesh out a broader Byzantine Mariology, there are a number of other sources one would need to consult. Mary's role is, of course, not one of mere theological abstraction. Mary is a real person, and, it is believed, she is a part of the Eastern Christian's day to day life. She appears not just in the liturgy, but in a number of other areas. Nonetheless, the liturgy is the central place for the expression of the Byzantine Church's beliefs.

Beyond the six feasts explored in this present work, however, a number of other areas should be consulted. These include other liturgical commemorations, non-liturgical hymnody, iconography, and legends and apparitions.

The lesser liturgical celebrations are usually associated with some legendary event, a relic, or a particular icon. So, for example, there is the popular feast of the Protection (*Pokrova*) of the *Theotokos* associated with her appearance in Constantinople

---

[215] Ibid., 107.

(1 October) and the commemoration of the Deposition of the Robe of the *Theotokos* in the Church at Blachernae (2 July).

There are, in addition, numerous iconographic representations of the Virgin. The symbolic content of these images is a valuable source of mariological information. There are many popular icons, e.g. that of Kazan, Czestochowa, the Joy of All Who Sorrow, the *Theotokos* of the Sign, the Virgin of Vladimir, "Sweet Kissing" (*Glykophylousa*), and the *Theotokos* of the Passion. In addition, there are many hundreds of lesser known icons, such as the *Theotokos* of the Burning Bush, the Inexhaustible Cup, the Milk-Giver, and the Abbess of Mt. Athos. Each of these images, and many others, is a legitimate source for understanding the Byzantine approach to the Mother of God. "Also to be considered is the highly developed cult of the commonly termed 'miraculous' icons of the *Theotokos*, some of which have given rise to important and extremely popular feasts."[216]

There is a multitude of marian prayers and hymnody that ought to be examined as well. The earliest extant marian prayer is the *Sub tuum praesidium*, traditionally dated to the third century, though Graef suggests it is a century later.[217] The hymn "It is truly proper to glorify you, O *Theotokos*," found its way from popular hymnody into the weekly celebration of the Eucharist, where it even "interrupts" the anaphora at the time of the commemoration of the saints. There is the Akathist hymn, penned by Saint Romanus the Melodist, which is used extensively throughout the Byzantine Churches, especially during Lent, usually in the context of Compline. And there is the Paraclesis service, an extended supplication to the Mother of God, that she intercede for the faithful. In addition, there are other shorter and longer hymns, both popular and liturgical. One, for example, is the Akathist to the Mother of God, Inexhaustible Cup and is associated with the icon of the same name.

---

[216] Bro. John Samaha, *Is There a Byzantine Mariology*. Online at: http://www.ewtn.com/library/LITURGY/BYZMARIO.TXT. Retrieved 9 December 2011. To these might be added, at least among Byzantine Christians in communion with Rome, the miraculous image of Guadalupe.
[217] Graef, 37.

All of these marian elements of the lived, experienced faith of the Byzantine Church must be taken into account in any full mariology. Nonetheless, it is still the liturgy that forms the core and structure of Eastern Christian life, and it is to the liturgical life that we most naturally turn to understand of the mysteries of the faith.

The *Theotokos* and Ever-Virgin Mary is a vitally important member of the communion of saints – and thus our Sister. She is the Mother of our God, and thus, in Christ, our Mother. She is the archetype of non-divine humanity, showing willing and ready submission to the will of God, which results in much spiritual fruit. She is the example of what a life "full of grace" is like. She is the eschatological sign of what redeemed humanity is to become. And she is a powerful intercessor who now, in the presence of God, prays for the salvation of the world.

Ultimately her value to the Christian believer is that she is one of us who leads the way ever deeper into the life in Christ.

> For Mary's vocation is also ours. Mary-*Theotokos* is called to bring her Son to birth in the hearts of us all. Is it our vocation to do any less? Mary, the Ark of the New Covenant, is a New Temple of God's dwelling among humankind. Is that not the vocation of all the baptized? ... Mary, like John the Baptist, was called to "prepare the way of the Lord." Are we called to any less?

> For Mary is not the only "God-bearer," any more than the pope is the only "Vicar of Christ," or that only the ordained share in Christ's priesthood of *leitourgia* (cf. 1 Pet 2:9), or that only deacons are called to *diakonia*, both of which mean service. These ministries exemplified for us by Jesus, Mary, the saints, and the liturgy of the Church, are the vocation of all the baptized.[218]

This is why the Byzantine Christian sings the honor of her name. The Lord has done great things for her and all generations will call her blessed (Lk 1.48-49). This is why we sing,

---

[218] Taft, 111-112.

It is truly proper to glorify you, O *Theotokos*, the ever-blessed, immaculate, and the Mother of our God. More honorable than the cherubim, and beyond compare more glorious than the seraphim, who a virgin gave birth to God the Word, you, truly the *Theotokos*, we magnify!

.

Bibliography

Adam, Adolf, *The Liturgical Year: It's History and It's Meaning After the Reform of the Liturgy*. Translated by Matthew J. O'Connell. New York: Pueblo Publishing Company, 1981.

Ancient Christian Commentary on the Scripture: New Testament III: Luke. Downers Grove, IL: InterVarsity Press, 2003.

Ancient Christian Commentary on the Scripture: New Testament VIII: Galatians, Ephesians, Philippians. Downers Grove, IL: InterVarsity Press, 1999.

Ancient Christian Commentary on the Scripture: New Testament X: Hebrews. Downers Grove, IL: InterVarsity Press, 2005.

Anderson, Jeffrey C., *The Byzantine Gospel Lectionary*, Introduction (University Park, PA: Penn State University Press, 1992.

Anglican-Orthodox Dialogue: The Dublin Agreed Statement 1984. Crestwood, NY: St. Vladimir's Seminary Press, 1985.

"Articles of Religion" in *The Book of Common Prayer* [1979]. New York: Church Hymnal Corporation, 1979.

Bavinck, Herman, *Reformed Dogmatics* (Vol. 4). Grand Rapids, MI: Baker Academic, 2008.

Bradshaw, Paul F. and Maxwell Johnson, *The Origins of Feasts, Fasts and Seasons in Early Christianity*. Collegeville, MN: Liturgical Press, 2011.

Bulgakov, Sergius, *The Burning Bush: On the Orthodox Veneration of the Mother of God*. Translated by Thomas Allan Smith. Grand Rapids, MI: Eerdmans, 2009.

Brown, Raymond, *The Birth of the Messiah: A Commentary on the Infancy Narratives in Matthew and Luke*. New York: Doubleday, 1977.

Calabuig, Ignazio M., OSM, "The Liturgical Cult of Mary in East and West" in *Handbook for Liturgical Studies Volume V: Liturgical Time and Space*. Collegeville, MN: Liturgical Press, 2000.

Calvin, John, *Institutes of the Christian Religion* (Vol. II), trans. Henry Beveridge. Grand Rapids, MI: Eerdmans, 1957.

Cassian, John, *Conferences*. New York: Paulist Press, 1985.

Catechism of the Catholic Church, The, 2nd ed. New York: Doubleday, 1995.

Comings, Jill Burnett, *Aspects of the Liturgical Year in Cappadocia (325-430)*. New York: Peter Lang, 2005.

Constas, Nicholas, *Proclus of Constantinople and the Cult of the Virgin in Late Antiquity: Homilies 1-5, Texts and Translations*. Boston: Brill, 2003.

DeSilva, David, *An Introduction to the New Testament: Contexts, Methods & Ministry Formation*. Downers Grove, IL: InterVarsity Press, 2004.

Divine Liturgies of Our Holy Fathers John Chrysostom and Basil the Great, The. Pittsburgh, PA: Byzantine Catholic Metropolitan Church *Sui Juris* of Pittsburgh, USA, 2006.

Dix, Gregory, *The Shape of the Liturgy*. New York: Seabury Press, 1982.

Gambero, Luigi, *Mary and the Fathers of the Church: The Blessed Virgin Mary in Patristic Thought*. Translated by Thomas Buffer. San Francisco: Ignatius Press, 1999.

Graef, Hilda, *Mary: A History of Doctrine and Devotion*. Notre Dame, IN: Ave Maria Press, 2009.

Fassler, Margot, "The First Marian Feast in Constantinople and Jerusalem: Chant Texts, Readings, and Homiletic Literature," in Peter Jeffrey, ed., *The Study of Medieval Chant: Paths and Bridges, East and West*. Rochester, NY: The Boydell Press, 2001.

First and Second Prayer Books of King Edward the Sixth, The. New York: E.P. Dutton & Co., nd.

Fuller, Reginald, Leonard Johnston and Conleth Kearns, *A New Catholic Commentary on the Scripture*. New York: Thomas Nelson, 1969.

Hahn, Scott, *Hail Holy Queen: The Mother of God in the Word of God*. New York: Doubleday, 2001.

Hapgood, Isabel Florence, *Service Book of the Holy Orthodox-Catholic Apostolic Church*, 3rd ed. Brooklyn, NY: Syrian Antiochian Orthodox Archdiocese, 1956.

Hennecke, Edgar, *New Testament Apocrypha* (Vol. 1), Wilhelm Schneemelcher, ed. Philadelphia: Westminster Press, 1963.

Hervieux, Jacques, *The New Testament Apocrypha*. Translated by Dom Wulstan Hibberd. New York: Hawthorn Books, 1960.

Hopko, Thomas, *Speaking the Truth in Love: The Entrance of the Theotokos Into the Temple*. Online at: http://ancientfaith.com/podcasts/hopko/ the_entrance_of_the_*theotokos*_into_the_temple. Retrieved 23 October 2011.

Katrij, Julian J., OSBM, *A Byzantine Rite Liturgical Year*. New York: Basilian Fathers Publications, 1983.

Kelly, Joseph, *The Origins of Christmas*. Collegeville, MN: Liturgical Press, 2004.

Lapham, Fred, *An Introduction to the New Testament Apocrypha*. New York: T&T Clark, 2003.

Ledit, Joseph, *Marie dans la liturgie de Byzance*. Paris: Éditions Beauchesne, 1976.

Luther, Martin, "Confession Concerning Christ's Supper – Part III," in *Martin Luther's Basic Theological Writings*. Timothy F. Lull, ed. Minneapolis, MN: Fortress Press, 2005.

Luther, Martin, "The Smalcald Articles," in *Martin Luther's Basic Theological Writings*. Timothy F. Lull, ed. Minneapolis, MN: Fortress Press, 2005.

Mary, Mother and Archimandrite Kallistos Ware, trans. *The Festal Menaion*. South Canaan, PA: St. Tikhon's Seminary Press, 1998.

Mateos, Juan, S.J., *Typicon de la Grande Eglise: Mss. (Timios Stauros 40)*. Rome: Pont. Institutum Orientalium Studiorum, 1962-3.

Meyendorff, John, *Byzantine Theology: Historical Trends and Doctrinal Themes*. New York: Fordham University Press, 1979.

Mills, David, *Discovering Mary: Answers to Questions About the Mother of God*. Cincinnati, OH: Servant Books, 2009.

Mills, William C., *Feasts of Faith: Reflections on the Major Feast Days*. Rollinsford, NH: Orthodox Research Institute, 2008.

Monk of the Eastern Church, A [Lev Gillet], *Orthodox Spirituality: An Outline of the Orthodox Ascetical and Mystical Tradition*. Crestwood, NY: St. Vladimir's Seminary Press, 1987.

New Interpreter's Bible, The, Vol. IX. Nashville, TN: Abingdon Press, 1995.

Payton, James, *Light from the Christian East: An Introduction to the Orthodox Tradition*. Downers Grove, IL: IVP Academic, 2007.

Pelikan, Jaroslav, *Mary Through the Centuries: Her Place in History and Culture*. New Haven, CT: Yale University Press, 1996.

Roberts, Alexander and James Donaldson, eds., *The Ante-Nicene Fathers: Translations of the Writings of the Fathers Down to A.D. 325*. (Vol. 8) Grand Rapids, MI: Eerdmans, 1989.

Roll, Susan K., *Toward the Origins of Christmas*. Kampen, The Netherlands: Kok Pharos Publishing House, 1995.

St. John Chrysostom, *The Cult of Saints*. Crestwood, NY: St. Vladimir's Seminary Press, 2006.

St. John of Damascus, *On the Divine Images*. Crestwood, NY: St. Vladimir's Seminary Press, 1980.

St. Theodore the Studite, *On the Holy Icons*. Crestwood, NY: St. Vladimir's Seminary Press, 1981.

Samaha, Bro. John, *Is There a Byzantine Mariology*. Online at: http://www.ewtn.com/library/LITURGY/BYZMARIO.T XT. Retrieved: 9 December 2011.

Shereghy, Basil, *The Liturgical Year of the Byzantine-Slavonic Rite*. Pittsburgh: Byzantine Seminary Press, 1968.

Taft, Robert F., SJ, "Marian Liturgical Veneration: Common Origins, Contemporary Catholic Renewal, and Meaning for Today," *Orientale Lumen III Conference 1999*. 15-18 June 1999.

Talley, Thomas J., *The Origins of the Liturgical Year*. New York: Pueblo Publishing Company, 1986.

Von Balthasar, Hans Urs, "Mary in the Church's Doctrine and Devotion," in Hans Urs von Balthasar and Joseph Cardinal Ratzinger, *Mary: The Church at the Source*. San Francisco: Ignatius Press, 1997.

Ware, Kallistos, *The Orthodox Way*, Revised Edition. Crestwood, NY: St. Vladimir's Seminary Press, 1995.

Ware, Timothy (Bishop Kallistos of Diokleia), *The Orthodox Church*, New Edition. New York: Penguin, 1997.

Warner, Marina, *Alone of All Her Sex: The Myth and Cult of the Virgin Mary*. New York: Alfred A. Knopf, 1976.

Wybrew, Hugh, *Orthodox Feasts of Christ and Mary: Liturgical Texts with Commentary*. London: SPCK, 1997.